THE COMPLEAT
ELVIS

Wise Publications
London/New York/Sydney

Exclusive Distributors
Music Sales Limited,
8/9 Frith Street,
London W1V 5TZ,
England.

Music Sales Pty. Limited,
120 Rothschild Avenue,
Roseberry,
NSW 2018,
Australia.

ISBN 0.86001-009.0
Order No. AM 1124 8

Art director: Pearce Marchbank
Designer: Paul May
Cover illustration: Philip Castle

Printed in England by
Redwood Books, Trowbridge, Wilts

Best Wishes
Elvis Presley

ELVIS

by Ray Connolly

On the evening of August 4, 1969, I found myself sitting in a corridor outside Elvis Presley's dressing room suite at the International Hotel, Las Vegas. I was positively terrified. Three nights earlier Elvis had confounded all critical speculation by making quite the most stunning return to live performing anyone could ever remember, and now I was to be granted an audience with the man every rock writer in the world wanted to meet. And Elvis, as we all knew so well, very, very rarely spoke to journalists. Then, as I sat there trying to remember one of the million questions I knew I had to ask, a strange thing happened, and I caught the only glimpse I was ever to get of Elvis Presley off guard. Very slightly the door to his dressing room fell open, and there sitting not six yards from me was the legend himself, quietly chatting with his aides, unaware of my embarrassed gaze. He was, I remember, suckling a bottle of Seven-Up, and he was thin and sleek in the black karate suit he had chosen for his stage comeback. Then above the drawl of conversation from inside the room I heard someone tell him that we were waiting outside. And suddenly, as if reacting to an instinctive need to preserve the glamour of his image he whipped a comb into his great jewelled right hand. And with his silver bracelets jingling and jangling and his left hand kneading and holding his black-dyed, non-slip and lately non-greased head, his right hand performed a semi-circular pompadour movement, which sent a wave of hair exploding across his skull and down his neck. And with a quick dab at those two black hairy spikes that cut deep into his cheeks, the legend was ready to receive. The repose had disappeared. The hair, the image, and the awesome public front of being the most famous entertainer in the world was repaired. Elvis was ready to talk to me. Not an Elvis in his mid-thirties: but a man who looked ten years younger, a man apparently petrified in time.

The door swung wide: "Elvis, I want you to meet Ray Connolly." The comb was gone, the body jerked off the couch, lines of practised welcome cracked by the eyes, and a dry, dark almost mahogany coloured hand reached out. "Hi, Ray," vibrated a billion dollars worth of larynx, and right there and then I was fifteen years old all over again.

That, to me, was one of the secrets of Elvis's massive appeal. His existence froze time. So long as he was alive we were all fifteen. And when he died reality caught up with all of us. In the weeks following his death I thought a great deal about that one meeting I had with him and about the shows I saw in the atmosphere of heady euphoria which pervaded Las Vegas during that month of August. I thought about the vitality of his performance, when nerves and energy had made him so slim and so anxious to please that he was arguably in the best shape he was ever to be as a singer. And I thought about how the insecurity he felt at facing a Las Vegas audience had forced him back on to the songs he knew he could do best, songs like 'Mystery Train', 'Trying to Get to You', and 'That's All Right, Mama'. But most of all I thought about our conversation, of how with cruel irony he joked about the minor weight problem which he had had during his nine years in Hollywood in the sixties, and how he believed that live performing was the cure for it. And then I thought about all the promises he made; plans which were all to come to nothing, as the impossible burden of being Elvis Presley was to finally weave its web into a stranglehold around him, a web which was to bind him even in death. He talked then of the plans he had for visiting parts of the world he had never seen, he promised again to visit Britain; he promised to make serious films and he promised to sing only songs to which he was truly committed. But somehow or other it all went wrong again. Wasn't he ashamed of the films and records he made during his years in Hollywood, I asked him, and I visibly felt the gasp of surprise in the room as his aides, the famous Memphis Mafia, looked on in shock at someone daring to criticise their employer to his face. For a moment Elvis looked shocked. And then becoming serious he said: "I wouldn't be being honest with you if I said I wasn't ashamed of some of the movies and the songs I've had to sing in them. I would like to say they were very good, but I can't. I've been extremely unhappy with that side of my career for some time. But how can you find twelve good songs for every film when you're making three films a year. I knew a lot of them were bad songs, and they used to bother the heck out of me. But I had to do them. They fitted the situation. I get more pleasure out of singing to an audience than any of the film songs have given me. How can you enjoy it when you have to sing to a guy you've just punched up.''

We all laughed because he wanted us to, and because we were glad that at last he seemed about to take a grip on his career. At least he recognised that for years he had been allowing silly trivia to hide his very real talents. We were not to know then that within a very short time he would have replaced poor films for half-hearted stage shows, and poor soundtrack albums for a whole succession of 'live' albums.

This book is only concerned with the music of Elvis Presley. To me everything else is irrelevant. Immediately after his death the publishing world threw out a noxious mass of scandalous trivia, much of which was conjectural, and all of which was meaningless in terms of the contribution which Presley made to the popular culture of our times. Personally I don't know whether or not Elvis Presley was heavily into drugs, occasionally sexually perverse or maniacally obsessed

ELVIS, AGED 6, WITH BLOND HAIR!

with violence and firearms. What I do know is that even if it is true it is also irrelevant.

The story of Elvis Presley has been told many times. In this book I want to re-tell it purely from the viewpoint of the music. Because whatever Elvis Presley may have become in terms of a world super-star, or revolutionary cultural figure, it is surely only the music which he created which has really any importance at all. When he died the London 'Times' in an absurd editorial commented that Elvis had an ''indifferent voice and sang for the most part poor songs.'' Apart from being a pointed insult at anyone who ever bought an Elvis Presley record, this was also about the most short-sighted comment that anyone could possibly have made about Elvis. Elvis Presley sang about emotion : and he sang with emotion. He was

THE PRESLEYS WITH ELVIS, AGED 8. BELOW: GRANDMOTHER MINNIE

the most popular singer of the last twenty one years because better than anyone else he was able to convey a wider variety of emotions in his singing. Technically there may have been other singers with truer tone, better controlled vibrato, better diction, and fewer personal nuances. But I can think of no-one who could wring so much emotion out of a single word, who could take a phrase and make it into an instantly personal testimony. Listen to the Presley version of 'Pieces of my Life' (1975) and you hear the total tragedy of the man as he sings with an abandonment of despair. Years ago, before Muhammad Ali regained his World Heavyweight Boxing crown, Elvis is reputed to have given him a gown with the words "People's Champion" embroidered on the back. The term might just as well have been applied in a musical sense to Elvis Presley. Because Elvis was in so many ways the people's champion of singing. Through his voice, through his records, we could relate to every emotion, from patriotism of 'American Trilogy' (1972) to the dejected loneliness of 'Loving Arms' (1974). He had a voice for all seasons, for all occasions. He was the embodiment of the music of the second half of the twentieth century, building upon the mainstream popular sounds of the thirties and forties created by Bing Crosby and his sound-alikes, and adding to it, in a truly momentous moment, a fusion of black rhythm and blues, white red necked country and western music, and, most importantly, the vigour and fervour of the gospel music which he cherished so much. Before Elvis, American popular music was spread across several different cultures, all loosely interconnected but all belonging to different races or classes of people. Elvis ended all of that. He was the great catalyst of popular music. At one of his first meetings with his first producer Sam Phillips he was asked what he could sing. "Anything," he replied. It was no idle boast. He could, and for the next twenty three years he did sing anything. And that was the attraction of Elvis. On his best albums he would juggle styles, going from blues,

ADOLESCENT ELVIS WITH COUSIN GENE SMITH

ELVIS, AGED 13, IN COWBOY SUIT

ELVIS AS A CADET AT HUME HIGH SCHOOL, MEMPHIS

to country to inspirationalist gospel, to ballads to soul and on to middle of the road pop without seeming to realise that he was pouring out all the ingredients which make up American (and therefore Western) popular music of today. And yet I don't think he ever realised just how important was his contribution to today's musical culture. He was never merely a singer taking off on a new tangent: musically he was a revolutionary. Sadly I suspect that the insularisation of his life must almost certainly have blinkered him to his own importance. When someone asked him in my presence to what he credited his phenomenal success he just shrugged and said that when he started there wasn't too much competition around. It would be much harder to make it now, he felt. He wasn't being overly modest. He really believed that. For some reason Elvis Presley, the man who changed the face of popular music for ever, and who provided raucous sensual anthems for the beginnings of a youth revolution which grew until it became the most important musical and art form of today, never knew what he had done. Perhaps the achievement was too much for any single person to be able to comprehend. Perhaps he was basically too humble of his own abilities, when there were others he admired so much. Or perhaps the people who surrounded him simply never realised either that the man they worked for was more, much more than merely a phenomenally successful singer. He may have been a revolutionary, but there was no-one there to tell him. And although virtually every rock artist to have followed him readily and happily admits to being primarily influenced by Presley, that too seems as though it was always too much for Elvis himself to comprehend.

If someone had wanted to create a pop cultural demi-God who would appeal to the widest number of people, create the biggest social storm and eventually make the most possible money, then that someone would have created Elvis Presley and set him down in Memphis, Tennessee in 1954. Only in hindsight can we see how perfectly assembled he was to become the biggest sociological myth of the middle of the twentieth century. In the past twenty three years we have grown totally accustomed to the idea of the basic four man rock group – the singer on rhythm guitar, the lead guitar, bass and drums. That was the line-up the Beatles presented and it provided a basic formula for creating a good full-blooded rock sound. But in 1954 when Presley began recording this kind of band had yet to be developed – and the original rock and roll sounds he recorded featured himself on acoustic guitar, Scotty Moore on the single electric guitar and Bill Black on the old fashioned string double bass, which required a station wagon roof-rack to carry it from gig to gig, and which could be used in either the orthodox fashion or as an improvised drum. D. J. Fontana wasn't to join the back-up band as a drummer until mid 1955.

Urban rhythm and blues, the field from which

TEENAGE ELVIS IN A LOCAL CADET FORCE

Presley took much of his early material, had been developing rapidly in the early fifties out of the rural negro blues songs, which when carried north to the cities by the migrant workers took on a new and more challenging form, but Presley, under the guidance of Sam Phillips of Sun Records was the man who neatly harnessed the new beat, and instead of playing it with the use of horns as the black musicians did, took the guitars of country music to interpret it. The result was that Elvis appealed to everyone, and fitted into all the classifications of music which then divided American pop. He was rhythm and blues, but he was white; and he was country and western although he sounded like a black man. Once the formula had been created he could hardly go wrong.

Elvis Aron Presley was born one of identical twins on January 8, 1935 (the other twin named Jesse Garon was stillborn) to a poor white Southern couple Gladys and Vernon Presley in a two roomed wooden hut in Tupelo, a small town in northeastern Mississippi. In

ELVIS, 18, WITH FATHER'S CAR

another age the "born-in-a-log-cabin" cliché might have been associated with aspirations in the political field, but Presley's own particular myth was to take him not towards Washington, but towards a fame more long-lasting and wide-spread than that of any politician. The wealth and the success which trailed him is a glorious example to those who see virtue in the "rags-to-riches-by-his-own-efforts" kind of story. And it's true Presley's beginnings typified virtually a text-book example of the mythical American folk hero.

It was in Tupelo that Elvis first became aware of music, when as a little blond boy (his hair had been dyed black since 1957) he would listen to the local radio stations and attend the Tupelo Evangelistic First Assembly of God church. It is ironical that when he later made excursions into hymns on his albums 'How Great Thou Art' and 'His Hand In Mine', etc., his performances met with scant respect from many who appreciated him as a rock singer, since it was in gospel music that much of the style which made rock possible was developed.

Years later in the mid-sixties when his recording career appeared to be going through a prolonged self-imposed doldrums it is interesting to note that for reasons known only to himself he should produce his best work only on a gospel session for the LP 'How Great Thou Art'. In my opinion gospel music is what Presley did best, since it was the one field to which he was totally committed, and the standard of his singing, the arrangements and recording of his gospel sessions would suggest that alone of all styles it was the one he took totally seriously.

Apart from gospel music, however, Elvis also grew up with country and western music, the songs of the southern white man, and the blues—the black man's music, and the influences on him by artists such as B. B. King, John Lee Hooker, Howlin' Wolf, Jimmy Reed and Arthur Big Boy Crudup was clear as soon as he began issuing records.

Professionally, Elvis's one single great opportunity came the day he was drawn to the attention of Sam Phillips, the head of the Sun Record Company in 1954. Elvis was 18 and a secretary who heard him sing was so impressed that she made a note of his name and telephone number. He might, she thought, be the singer Sam Phillips had been looking for.

If today's music owes a lot to Elvis Presley then it owes maybe just a little bit more to Sam Phillips. As the owner of the tiny Sun label Phillips has been unquestionably the most important record producer in the history of pop. In the early fifties he began a career in the record industry by recording blues artists and leasing the tapes to bigger companies like Chess in Chicago. He was a white man fascinated by blues, and he was always on the look out for a white man who could sing with the soul of a blues singer. That man eventually turned out to be Presley.

At first Phillips wasn't too sure about Presley's appeal

ELVIS, HIS COUSIN AND THEIR TWO DATES AT A HIGH SCHOOL PROM

ABOVE LEFT: SUN RECORDS' BOSS, SAM PHILLIPS

LEFT: ELVIS AND HIS FIRST MANAGER BOB NEAL

ABOVE: THE FIRST GOLD RECORD

(and in later years Elvis would always remind people that it was actually the secretary, Marion Keisker, who urged Sam Phillips to give Elvis a chance), but he was interested enough to encourage him to rehearse over a period of several weeks with a couple of sympathetic, although initially unenthusiastic Memphis musicians, Scotty Moore on electric guitar and Bill Black on string bass. And eventually in the June of 1954 he decided to start recording. The first track put down was 'I Love You Because' (which Phillips didn't think worth releasing but which RCA were to put on to their first Presley album), and the session seems to have been particularly uninspired until someone came upon the idea of covering Big Boy Crudup's 'That's All Right, Mama' . . . a blues song initially recorded by Crudup in 1947.

Still unsure of himself Elvis resolved any problems he may have had with his styling by copying the original recording almost note-for-note, breath-for-breath. (This was not to be the last time that Presley stole styles : on another blues song 'Reconsider Baby' on the album Elvis is Back made in 1960 he stuck so closely to the Lowell Fulson original recording that had it not been such a remarkably good record it would have been embarrassing, while several of his gospel songs such as 'Working On The Building' bear more than a passing resemblance to the original arrangements performed by his friends The Blackwood Brothers gospel singers.)

For the flip side of 'That's All Right, Mama' the hillbilly Bill Monro song 'Blue Moon of Kentucky' was chosen, thus coupling blues with country and western, a precedent which Phillips was to stick to during Elvis's next sixteen months with Sun Records. Excited about the sound he had created Sam Phillips was, however, unsure of where to place the record since at that time there was a pretty rigid race distinction between the types of records played on Memphis radio stations, and he felt that the white stations would veto it because it was too black in sound, and the black ones wouldn't be interested because it was by a white man. Eventually he decided to try an old friend Dewey

NOVEMBER 1955: ELVIS SIGNS FOR RCA.

BELOW: BREAKFAST WITH ELVIS

Phillips (no relation) a white disc jockey who played blues records on his programme.

'That's All Right, Mama' was played over the air for the first time at around 9.30 on the evening of July 3. Public reaction was instantaneous, and within a few days Sam Phillips had a small local hit on his hands. (Although the record was, in one form or another to one day become a half-million seller for RCA Victor, it never did cause much more than a small ripple of interest around Memphis when first recorded. The flip side, 'Blue Moon of Kentucky', got a few plugs on a local country and western station, but had little impact.)

At this time Elvis Presley was a 6ft. tall nineteen year old youth, with a strong Memphis accent, furry, post adolescent sideburns, a touch of acne, and fair-to-brown long greasy hair, cut in the style of Tony Curtis, which allowed a pompadour to fall over his eyes when he shook his head. Wearing his favourite colours of pink and black he was vain and he was flash. But he was handsome and exciting, and when he sang up-beat numbers he allowed his body to move to the rhythm. At first there is little doubt that his stage movements were spontaneous, but as soon as he realised their value in whipping up an audience, no performance was complete without a series of contrived pelvic contortions, which were later to earn him the nick-name Elvis the Pelvis, and to become virtually as famous as his voice.

During the next few months Elvis, with Bill Black and Scotty Moore, toured all over the South, taking gigs where they could get them. By this time he'd given up his short career as a truck driver – although after his first live radio gig on the Grand Ole Opry show he was advised by the MC there to go back to truck driving – and he was continuing to make records for Sam Phillips. On the following sessions Phillips was to guide him through 'Good Rockin' Tonight', backed with 'I Don't Care If The Sun Don't Shine' and 'Milk Cow Blues Boogie' backed with 'You're A Heartbreaker'. All the time his reputation was growing, and the excitement of the crowds was spreading, but it was only after his fourth single, released in May 1955, and coupling the hiccuping, echoing 'Baby, Let's Play House' with 'I'm Left, You're Right, She's Gone' that his style really became set, and that he really began to move towards the big time. On this record it is noticeable that for the first time a drummer has been added to the line-up, D. J. Fontana, and the music now takes on a harder, bluesier feel to it.

By now Elvis was news all over the South and had been drawn to the attention of the self styled 'Colonel' Tom Parker, a former manager of Johnny Cash and one-time fairground barker. Moving with a Machiavellian diplomacy Parker proceeded to convince Presley's parents that their son ought to become involved with a much bigger organisation which would be able to make better use of his talents. That organisation turned out to be RCA Victor Records, and in November 1955 it was publicly announced that Sam Phillips had sold Presley's contract for 35,000 dollars,

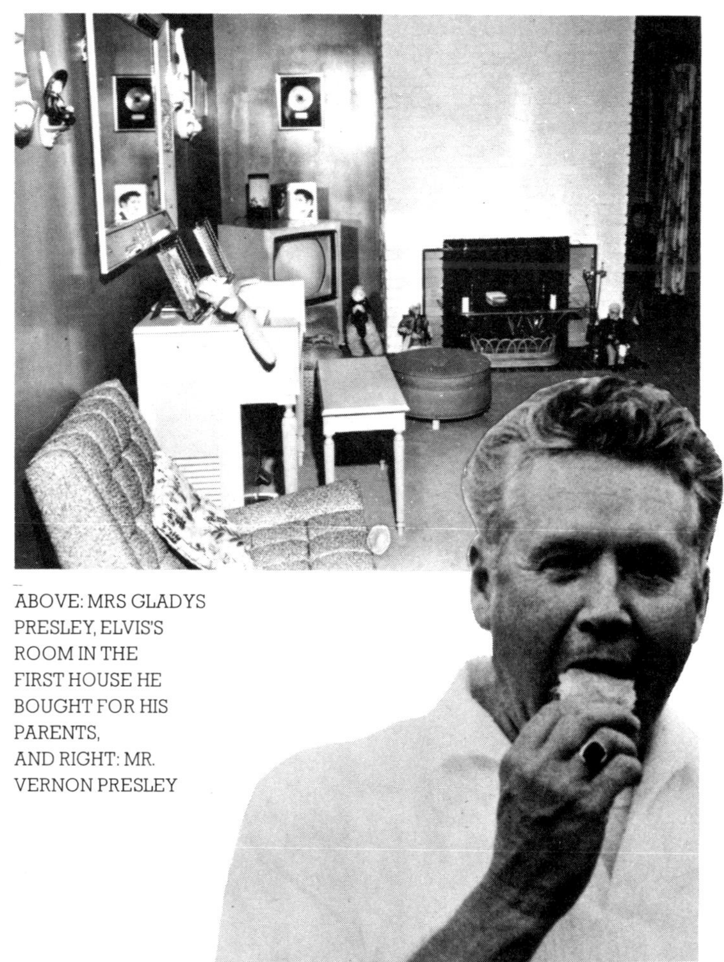

ABOVE: MRS GLADYS PRESLEY, ELVIS'S ROOM IN THE FIRST HOUSE HE BOUGHT FOR HIS PARENTS, AND RIGHT: MR. VERNON PRESLEY

1958: ABOVE: ARMY BOUND ELVIS SAYS GOODBYE TO PARENTS, AND RIGHT: TO CO-STAR DOLORES HART AND FRIEND VALERIE ALLEN.

promising RCA the right to all of Elvis's released and unreleased material. Of the fifty or so tapes that RCA acquired, only ten had been previously issued, but within the next few months they were to release a further five – 'I Love You Because', 'I'll Never Let You Go', 'Blue Moon', 'Just Because' and 'Trying to Get To You'. (We had to wait another sixteen years for 'Harbour Lights' and an alternate version of 'I Love You Because'.)

And ever since 1956 it has been a bone of some major contention among Presley fanatics, of whom there are thousands, that RCA have not issued all of the available Sun recordings and a continuing lobby has been kept up by the fan clubs for the release of 'Tennessee Saturday Night', 'Uncle Pen', 'My Baby's Gone' (which is now available on a pirate record), 'Last Train to Memphis' and 'Gone'.

Had Sam Phillips settled for a smaller transfer fee and insisted on retaining his rights to the records he had produced he would undoubtedly have made millions out of Elvis, but at that time he was hardly to know that he had discovered the man, and produced the sound which was to change the world's conception of pop music. As it was he quickly turned his attention to other artists, and during the next few years had incredible success with Carl Perkins, Jerry Lee Lewis, Johnny Cash and to a lesser extent Charlie Rich and Roy Orbison. And these singers possessed something which Presley did not: not only did they play and sing, they also wrote their own material. Despite Presley's name on several early songs he never actually composed anything.

By the time he joined RCA at the end of 1955 he was already a slight celebrity in the Southern States, with his pink Cadillacs and erotic act, and had even had several singles on the national country and western charts, but it was his first Victor single 'Heartbreak Hotel' which was to stamp his personality indelibly upon the world.

'Heartbreak Hotel' was recorded in the January of 1956 in Nashville. Already Presley's style was developing away from the Sam Phillips sound which had made him, and now a piano had been added to take over from the guitar during the instrumental break. This was the record that was to make rockers of us all. The echo was shattering in its impact, and the raw aggressiveness of the guitar work was jolting in its recurrent insistence.

In America the record shot to the top of the charts, helped undoubtedly by the tactics of Colonel Parker who had pulled off the impossible by getting his discovery on to several networked television shows. Middle-class America had never seen anything quite like Elvis in their living rooms before, and the conservative right wing began anti-Elvis campaigns, in which he was burnt in effigy by the girls from a New York convent, while serious articles were written about this new threat to the morals of the young. With

Thanks
Elvis

ELVIS AT THE GATES OF HIS MEMPHIS HOME...

superb handling Parker continually traded on the backlash, and went so far as to get Elvis to sing in one show standing rigidly still as though he were in a straitjacket. Presley was having maximum exposure, and it all added up to gigantic record sales, and masses of headlines. During his first year with RCA four million selling singles were issued – 'Heartbreak Hotel', 'I Want You, I Need You, I Love You', 'Don't Be Cruel' backed with 'Hound Dog' and 'Love Me Tender'. For a dollar any fan could buy a little chunk of Elvis.

By this time he was recording some of the current Rhythm and Blues hits of the period, all with a direct and raucous urgency, and one of them 'Blue Suede Shoes' was to be a bigger hit in Britain for him than it was for the composer Carl Perkins. (Other R and B songs recorded at that time were 'Money Honey', 'Tutti Frutti', 'I Got A Woman', 'Shake Rattle & Roll', 'Lawdy Miss Clawdy' and 'Blueberry Hill'.)

In Britain 'Don't be Cruel' was his biggest hit of the year. In October 'Blue Moon' was issued as a single and that made the charts, too, to be followed within a couple of months by both 'Love Me Tender' and 'Love Me', a track from his second LP. which as an extended play record had sold a million in the States. But the initial excitement generated by his early records was beginning to diminish outside America. Although his next release, 'Too Much', went straight to the top of the charts in the States, in the UK. it only got as far as thirteenth position before beginning its downward trend.

The next release in the summer of 1957 changed everything – and 'All Shook Up' became his first of a long series of number one hits all over the world. In America fans had been able to see Presley in action on television and on his tours, but to the European fans the Presley act was something they read about in newspapers. Admittedly he'd had one film released, 'Love Me Tender', but in it his movements had been pretty restricted, and it wasn't until his second film 'Loving You' that his European following began to understand exactly what all the hysteria was about. Here was an idol who looked the way every young man might want to look in 1957, and who represented what every girl wished her boy-friend to be. And by the time his third film 'Jailhouse Rock', came out, at the end of 1957 he was as big in Britain, Europe, and probably just about everywhere in the world as he was in America.

But already his career had been through several changes musically. With Sun Records he had sung blues and hillbilly music; RCA's studios in Nashville had added a vocal backing, The Jordanaires, heard for the first time on 'Heartbreak Hotel', and had begun to trade upon some of his mannerisms. Thus, by the time 'Too Much' came out he was a mannered and contrived singer, coming on harder on the backbeat, and generally drifting away from his early blues field.

Already Elvis was relying, more and more upon writers contracted to his music publishers, Hill and Range, to provide him material, and he began to record more and more songs by Otis Blackwell and the brilliant Jerry Leiber and Mike Stoller. Of all his associations with writers the one he had with Jerry Leiber and Mike Stoller would appear to have been the most artistically rewarding, in that they seemed to be able to capture the meanness that he generated ('Trouble') while also being capable of writing witty and amusing lyrics (read those to 'Jailhouse Rock'). Every time a Presley recording session was due teams

...AND IN THE GARDEN

of writers would be asked to submit material for consideration which would then be conveyed to Presley via Freddy Bienstock his music publisher, and the nearest thing Presley has ever had to an old fashioned A & R man.

The Presley Phenomenon was moving rapidly away from its roots, and becoming a carefully packaged commodity. By now he had already shown his interest in hymns with the release of 'Peace In The Valley', and conservative commercialism with his first Christmas album, but the singles were beginning to come with a chart topping monotony . . . 'Teddy Bear', 'Jailhouse Rock', 'Don't' and 'I Beg Of You'. Then in 1958 the impossible happened.

Elvis was drafted into the United States Army. In America the effect was cataclysmic, and some idea of the trauma that the event must have had can be gauged if one figures what the reaction would have been among English fans had Paul McCartney been called up in 1966. Before joining the Army Elvis had been wise enough to record a small stockpile of material for release in single form during his two years away, including 'Wear My Ring Around Your Neck' and 'Hard Headed Woman' (from his latest film 'King Creole'). And then during his first leave he cut some more sides in Nashville including 'I Got Stung', 'One Night', 'A Fool Such As I' and 'Big Hunk Of Love'. But by June of 1959 the stockpile had come to an end, claimed RCA, and there were to be no further releases. In actual fact there were several titles which had not yet been issued and which were to appear in later years, including 'Ain't That Loving You Baby' and 'Tell Me Why'. But probably in 1959 neither RCA nor the Colonel considered these titles strong enough for single release, and it wasn't until Presley fell into the dull monotony of making film albums in the mid-sixties that they were considered to be of any great value.

The army changed everything for Elvis. Before he was inducted he was the perpetual rebel, sexually blatant and increasingly vulgar in his taste of clothes and cars. But with the shaving of the side-burns, and the re-emergence of the tawny hair his personality changed. To make matters worse (so far as young people were concerned) he turned out to be the model soldier (no rebellious Muhammad Ali he), and shortly after his return to civilian life in 1960 it became clear that the days of riots, hysteria and charges of obscenity were over. His first release stuck very much to the lurching rockabilly sound he'd built up before the army ('Stuck On You') and sold just as well as everyone thought it would, and his first album was superb in its range of material and the execution of so

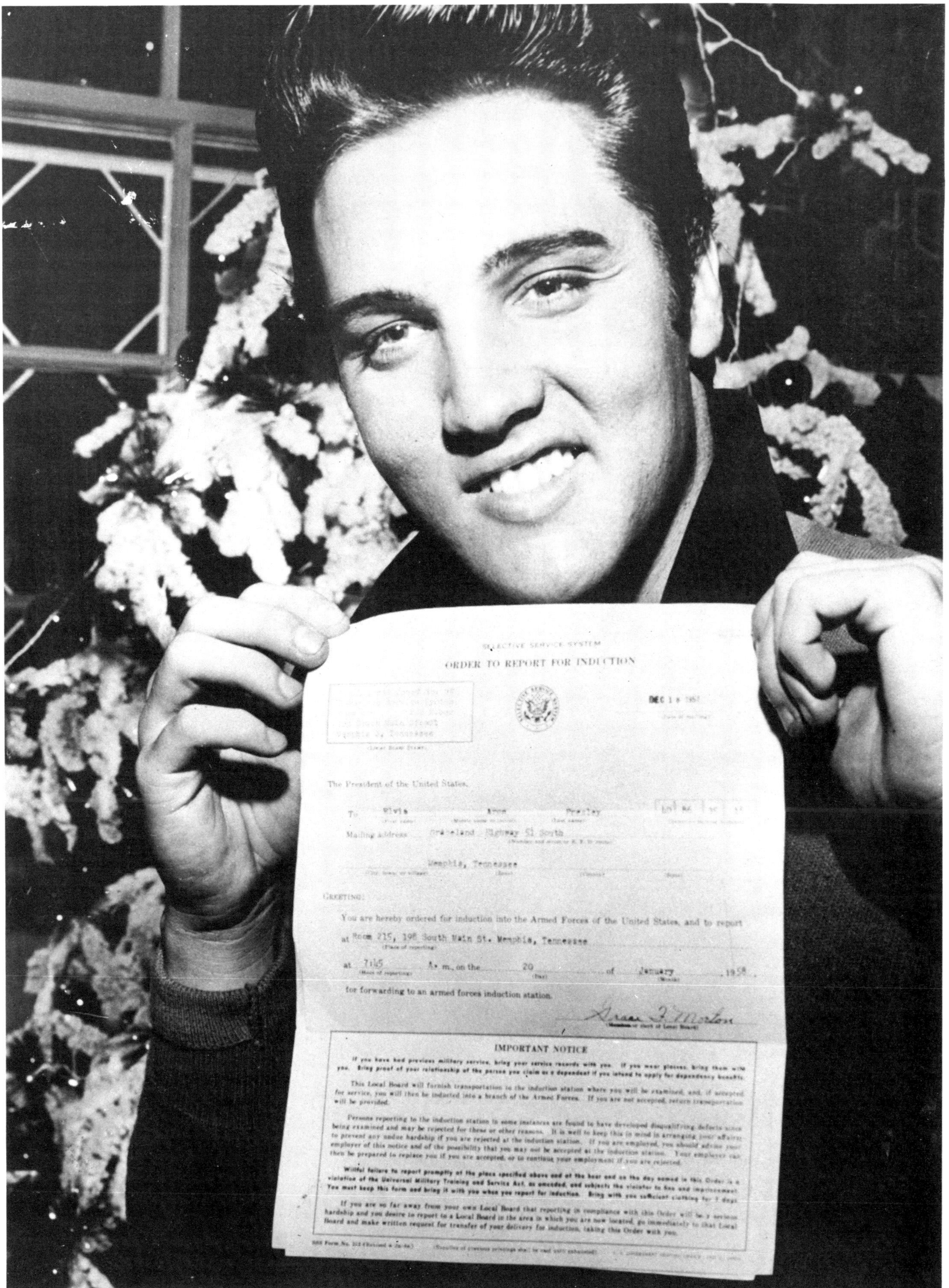
SELECTIVE SERVICE SYSTEM
ORDER TO REPORT FOR INDUCTION
Memphis, Tennessee
The President of the United States,
To Elvis Aron Presley
Mailing address Graceland Highway 51 South
Memphis, Tennessee
GREETING:
You are hereby ordered for induction into the Armed Forces of the United States, and to report
at Room 215, 198 South Main St. Memphis, Tennessee
at 7:45 A. m., on the 20 of January, 1958
for forwarding to an armed forces induction station.
IMPORTANT NOTICE

SPEARHEAD

1959: THE ARMY LEVELS ALL... LEFT: PRISCILLA BEAULIEU, AGED 16. CENTRE LEFT: ELVIS AT GRACELANDS; CENTRE RIGHT: IN A SCENE FROM G.I. BLUES. BOTTOM LEFT: ELVIS WITH ARMY FRIENDS AND, BOTTOM RIGHT, ELVIS AND FATHER

TOP: IN A SCENE FROM KID GALAHAD WITH JOAN BLACKMAN AND LOLA ALBRIGHT. ABOVE: A SCENE FROM GIRLS, GIRLS, GIRLS. RIGHT: ELVIS WITH TUESDAY WELD IN WILD IN THE COUNTRY

many varying styles. And in Britain one of the cuts, 'Girl Of My Best Friend', became one of his biggest hits ever (1960 and 1976), being backed with the excellent Doc Pomus/Mort Shuman song 'Mess Of Blues'. Once when I asked Mort Shuman about his relationship with Presley he denied that it ever existed, despite the fact that he wrote several hits for him ('Little Sister', 'His Latest Flame', 'Suspicion', 'Kiss Me Quick', 'Surrender' and 'She's Not You'). "We'd just hear that he was short of songs and write a few and send them down to Nashville for him. I remember they telephoned right from the studio one night because they couldn't get the introduction to 'His Latest Flame' right. So I explained, and still they got it wrong. He made me a lot of money, and I think I helped him make some, but he never did phone to thank me for the songs."

Between 1960 and 1963 Presley worked non-stop, the films coming at the rate of three a year, 'G.I. Blues',

GIRLS, GIRLS, GIRLS

'Flaming Star' (his best ever acting performance), 'Wild In The Country', 'Follow That Dream', 'Blue Hawaii', 'Kid Galahad', 'Girls, Girls, Girls', 'Fun In Acapulco' and 'Viva Las Vegas' . . . and his recording career prospered like never before, with the former Caruso song 'O Sole Mio' being retitled 'It's Now Or Never' and finally selling over eight million copies, one of the best selling singles ever by anyone. But Elvis had changed. The sideboards were gone : he was a far wider entertainer now, as illustrated on his own personal favcurite record 'Are You Lonesome Tonight'. His first full album of spirituals, 'His Hand In Mine', released in Britain in 1961, illustrated that he'd lost none of his capabilities, but his singles were now rounded off, smoothed out versions of what he had been doing three years ago. All the same 'Surrender' sold well, 'I Feel So Bad' was an excellent rendition of the Chuck Willis R and B song (although in Britain it was a flip side and 'Wild In The Country' topped the charts) and 'I Can't Help Falling In Love With You' was to eventually become a standard. The albums 'Something For Everybody' and 'Pot Luck' accentuated that he was now aiming at a larger audience, and the dropping of the now expected echo chamber on most of the tracks, the lack of gutsy guitar and the introduction of the even-then old fashioned saxophone only tended to soften the voice which had originally been noticeable for its harshness and for its aggression. Hits now came out of the studios regularly every three months – 'Good Luck Charm', being followed by 'She's Not You', and then 'Return To Sender'.

But then in 1963 for the first time since almost anyone could remember Elvis failed to make the number one position when 'One Broken Heart For Sale' ran into trouble halfway down the Top Twenty and then disappeared. In between 'Return To Sender' and 'Broken Heart' something had happened to pop : the Beatles had arrived and were now ruling the roost with first 'Please, Please Me' and then 'From Me To You'. Compared to the enthusiastic sound the Beatles were creating Elvis was now beginning to sound too smooth, and too contrived for the fans. Possibly aware of this position he returned to the studios in March of that year and came out with 'Devil in Disguise', which while hitting the top spots in both Britain and America did little to help repair his slipping image. 'Bossa Nova Baby' which followed could have been one of his good records, since the beat, words, performance and organ breaks were genuinely exciting, but the performance was ruined by a dreadful instrumental break which sounded like a Saturday night in a Mexican brothel. It may have fitted in with the situation in the film it was from, but it should have been re-recorded for release as a single.

Between the end of 1963 and the end of 1967 there's very little that can be said about Presley's artistic career. Almost as if he were purposely secluding himself and avoiding any confrontation with the Beatles, he worked steadily in Hollywood churning out cheap witless films one after the other. On the recording side his career plummeted. Admittedly his singles still sold reasonably well, but this was surely due to his enormous fan following rather than to any special merit. Mostly he put out poor albums, containing eight or so dreadful situation film songs, and also a couple of so-called 'bonus' tracks. Ironically most of the best tracks he was to record during this crass and dull mid-sixties period were to be titled 'bonus' tracks, and generally thrown away on the flip side of albums. For instance on Spinout in 1966 we find three excellent tracks tucked away so that neither disc jockeys nor public might notice them . . . 'Tomorrow Is A Long Time', a Bob Dylan song, which Dylan admits is the favourite version of any of his songs ever recorded, the old Clover's hit 'Down In The

MPP122901-12/29-MEMPHIS,TENN.: DECKED OUT IN A MOD BLACK FUR SUIT,
ENTERTAINER ELVIS PRESLEY WALKS FROM HALL AFTER SERVIG AS BEST MAN AT THE
WEDDING OF DELBERT WEST,JR., PRESLEY'S CHIEF SECURITY OFFICER, HERE 12/28.
PRESLEY ALSO CARRIES A FLASHLIGHT AND WEARS A GOLD MEDALLION AS PART OF THE
"METALLIC ACCESSORIES" OF HIS OUTFIT. (UPI) 211 (sp)

Alley' and a beautifully pretty song 'I'll Remember You', all of which were recorded with considerably more attention than any of the rest of the album. Similarly the flip side of 'Kissin' Cousins' (the single) carried the strong and dynamic song 'It Hurts Me'.

In 1965 in the midst of the film albums a hotchpotch of left over songs Elvis For Everyone was issued, which included among the dross, a version of 'Memphis', 'Tennessee', and two other good songs 'Tomorrow

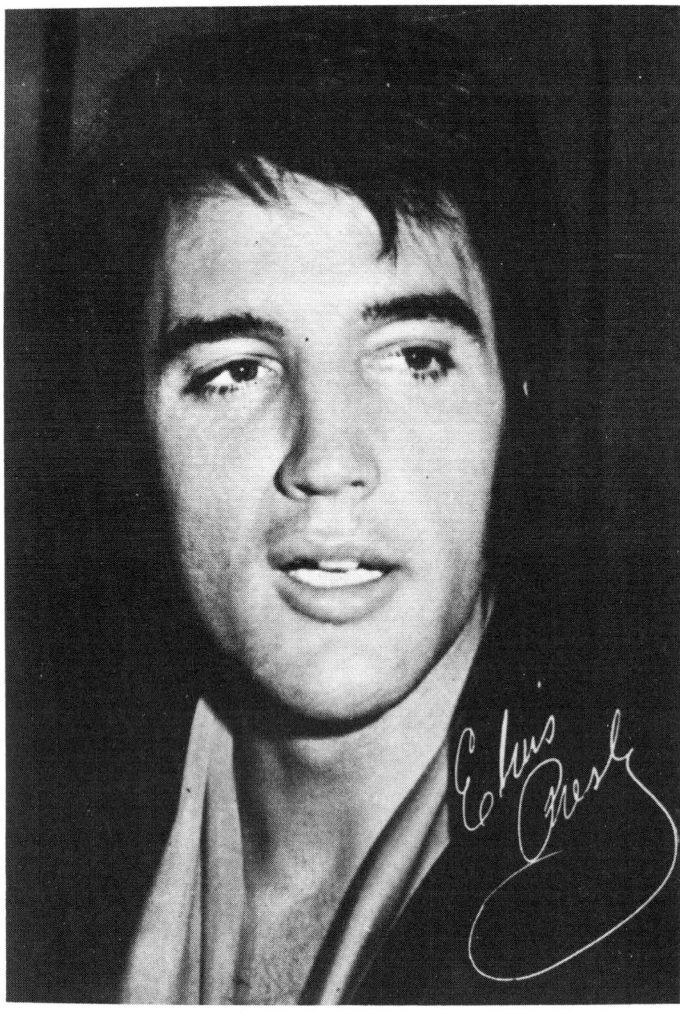

Night' and 'I Met Her Today'. These may not have been the best things Elvis ever did, but they were certainly 100 per cent better than his film albums. Attempts to fathom the mind and attitudes of Presley during this very lean period of his artistic career are virtually futile. He could be excused for the films he made, since he always held reservations about his acting talents, but there are no plausible explanations for his erratic recording career, and the even more erratic packaging processes that went along with it. Even the cover pictures on the records seemed to bear no relation to the mystical figure of the fifties, or to the new styles of the sixties. He looked plump, camp and bored, and while the Beatles and Stones generated excitement all over the world, never allowing their records to be less than interesting, Elvis seemed to retreat further behind his group of aides and bodyguards. Possibly he was wise in not taking on the Beatles and the Stones at their own game, because he could only have come off second best. His days of hysteria from the pre-adolescents were over, and he hadn't yet begun to reap the harvest of being the man who started it all. Possibly he was tired and bored with the whole routine, ground down by the seemingly endless chain of movies. Also by this time he must have found himself in a situation where he was never criticised. The Memphis Mafia were good friends, but they were 'yes-men'. He could never expect an honest assessment of his performances from them, or from anybody else, and if the records were not selling in quite the quantities that they once had done, nevertheless the gold records continued to pile up. With the fans Elvis has never been able to do wrong: if his career has had its bad moments then that is the responsibility of the Colonel, MGM pictures or RCA Victor Records.

But all bad spells must inevitably sometime come to an end, and perhaps coincidentally it was marriage to Priscilla Beaulieu in May 1967 that marked the change in his fortunes. Elvis and Priscilla had met while she was still a schoolgirl when Elvis was in Germany, and though she had gone to stay in his house when she returned to the States, Elvis continued to enjoy other girls in Hollywood. When the marriage came it was a shock to everyone, but bigger shocks were in store. Just a few months later Elvis was back at the RCA studios in Nashville and the first track he recorded was the Jimmy Reed standard blues song 'Big Boss Man'. At the same session he also cut a Jerry Reed song 'Guitar Man', which sounded strangely autobiographical, and was reckoned to be his best single in years, backed with another blues number 'High Heel Sneakers'. Just as Sam Phillips had demonstrated twelve years before Elvis was at his best when coupling blues with country and western. Now Elvis was back in the charts, and new fans were showing interest. 'U.S. Male' followed, a real red-neck Southern song almost in talking hillbilly blues style, by Jerry Reed, and the pattern was being set.

Then in the summer of 1968 a new stage in the Presley career was begun when it was determined that he should make a spectacular for NBC, his first televised performance since he appeared with Frank Sinatra in Miami, Florida in 1960 shortly after he left the army. The reasons for his return to television were, in the Colonel's eyes, because he was now unable to command the million dollars a picture he had during most of the sixties, and the deal offered by NBC made very

ELVIS PRESLEY

ABOVE AND BELOW: THE ELVIS SPECIAL TV SHOW

sound economic sense. The result was a strange programme, a mixture of Elvis doing what he does best, that is playing and singing most of his early hits with a group of his favourite musicians. The informality and the freshness with which he approached songs he'd first performed ten, twelve and thirteen years earlier suggested that he was no longer to be a puppet of financial manipulators. Some critics dismissed the show as being dated, but they were wrong and short-sighted. The strength of that kind of performance is that it can never date : the progressive rock groups may have begun to do things that Elvis and his band wouldn't even begin to know existed, but there he was, in person, laying down the roots from where it all sprang. If Elvis singing 'Lawdy, Miss Clawdy' is dated musically, so are the roots to any folk art form. Some of the more contrived sections of the show were, however, less successful, particularly the 'Big Boss Man' routine, which apart from ruining the song, looked like a scene from one of his beach films, but generally speaking the programme confirmed dramatically that even after all these years the man was still stacked with style, and still capable of singing with that earthy sexiness that had opened the flood gates of rock.

To finish the show he sang a vaguely protest song 'If I Can Dream' which became his first million selling single for several years. Obviously excited by reactions to his television special Elvis went back to

COLONEL TOM PARKER

ABOVE: THE COLONEL AND ELVIS MEET THE MAYOR OF MEMPHIS

serious recording, and in the January of 1969 he returned to Memphis to cut 36 titles at the American Recording Studios, under the supervision of Chips Moman, who had supervised hits for the Box Tops, Dusty Springfield, Joe Tex and Dionne Warwick within the preceding few months. In terms of quality and output it was probably the best recording session Elvis has ever done, providing enough material for two albums ('Elvis in Memphis' and 'Back In Memphis') as well as several hits, including 'In The Ghetto', 'Suspicious Minds', 'Don't Cry Daddy' and 'Kentucky Rain'. What American Studios got out of Presley during the six days of non-stop recording was the soul and the perfectionism that he had been lacking in so many of his Nashville and Hollywood sessions. And the choice of songwriters was wider than any he'd tried in years – from Lennon and McCartney to Burt Bacharach, Neil Diamond, Mac David and John Hartford.

By the time 'In The Ghetto' became his next million seller it had been announced that Elvis was to do a month's stint at a brand new Las Vegas night club at the International Hotel. And that was where I finally caught up with him in person after following his career so closely for so many years.

Elvis in 1969 was thin and very nervous. He was afraid that the Las Vegas audience might laugh at him, and as a confidence booster he begged all of his old

friends to fly out to Las Vegas for the opening night. Sam Phillips, the man who fourteen years earlier had discovered him, was at first reluctant to go : ''I explained to Elvis when he called that I had business to take care of here in Memphis, but he kept on asking me. He wanted advice, too. I told him that whatever he did he mustn't let them surround him with one of those big Las Vegas type orchestras, and that the best thing he could do was to get the best set of musicians around him he could find . . . musicians who played his kind of music. He said that was what he was going to do, but he still kept on asking me to fly out there for his first night. He was that unsure of himself. So in the end I just took off there to be with him.''

For Elvis it was the vital test, and anyone who has seen the two films of Elvis on stage – 'That's The Way It Is' and 'Elvis On Tour' – must now know that whatever his limits as a film actor may have been, he appeared to have a virtually unlimited ability to communicate with an audience – a strange irony, since so many of his personal relationships ended fraught and unhappily. As a performer I'm inclined to the belief that Elvis was possibly at his best during those first few visits to Las Vegas and the short tours which followed in 1970. He had graduated from the adolescent rebellious rock figure of his first success into a far more rounded performer, and at last he was able to demonstrate just how far the natural talents he had always possessed could be stretched when harnessed to the appropriate material.

After his triumphant return to live performing Elvis could seemingly do no wrong and a long string of hits followed. But he never again managed to reach that peak of sustained energy which had characterised his return to recording in Memphis, and before long the standard of some of his work was again slipping as the challenge went out of recording. There were however million sellers taken from other sessions, 'The Wonder of You', 'I've Lost You' and 'You Don't Have to Say You Love Me', but now it seemed that the market was being swamped with so many Presley records that he couldn't possibly be taking them all seriously. He was caught in his old trap. Success had returned to him with such enormity that it hardly seemed worth the effort to live up to his name. All the same there were some very good records, including a cover of the B. J. Thomas hit 'Just Can't Help Believing', which was a live recording from the film That's The Way It Is, the American number one rocker 'Burning Love', and the moving 'American Trilogy', which was featured in the second Elvis 'on stage' movie 'Elvis On Tour'.

But in 1972 something happened to him which was to change the last years of his life and ironically was, I believe, to bring him to make some of his best records. Elvis and his wife Priscilla split up. The effects would appear to have been totally shattering to his ego, but he turned it into his music. Where he had once sung about the joy of unfettered youth with more than a hint of wilful carnality, he now began to choose songs which appeared to depict his own personal state. Thus the records became lonely appeals from the heart, as though he were trying to get over his divorce by singing about it. Musically the effects were emotionally wrenching. In 1972 came 'Always On My Mind', in 1974 there was 'My Boy' and 'Loving Arms', in 1975 'Pieces of My Life', in 1976 was 'Hurt', while in the last year of his life he recorded the very moving song by Tim Rice and Andrew Lloyd Webber 'It's Easy For You'. At the same time his stage act was extended to bring in songs like 'My Way', 'Lord, You Gave Me A Mountain' and 'There Goes My Everything'. Not that he gave up rock and roll completely. I particularly liked his version of Tony Joe White's 'I've Got A Thing About You Baby' and Chuck Berry's 'Promised Land', while 'Steamroller Blues', 'Trouble' and 'Way Down' were all indications that he had lost none of his magic with rhythmical material.

No-one who had followed Presley's career carefully could have been surprised at his death on August 16, 1977. It was well-known that he had been unwell for some time, and the exhausting series of concerts to which he submitted himself can hardly have helped matters. (He played over 100 cities in the last year of his life.) As it was the most loved singer on earth was to die a lonely man whose sole pleasure was in performing to the people who had grown up with the sound of his voice in their ears.

I said earlier in this preface that while Elvis lived we were all fifteen. But maybe his influence will go further than that. So long as his records continue to be played a part of us will always be young.

DISCOGRAPHY

A complete list of every Elvis Presley album available in the United Kingdom.

1956 : ROCK 'N' ROLL SF 8233
Blue suede shoes : I got a sweetie (I got a woman) : I'm counting on you : I'm left, you're right, she's gone : That's all right : Money honey : Mystery train : I'm gonna sit right down and cry over you : Trying to get to you : One-sided love affair : Lawdy, Miss Clawdy : Shake, rattle and roll

1956 : ELVIS (ROCK 'N' ROLL No. 2) SF 7528
Rip it up : Love me : When my blue moon turns to gold again : Long tall Sally : First in line : Paralysed : So glad you're mine : Old Shep : Ready Teddy : Any place is paradise : How's the world treating you : How do you think I feel

1957 : LOVING YOU PL 42358
Mean woman blues : Teddy bear : Loving you : Hot dog : Party : Gotta lot of livin' to do : Lonesome cowboy : True love : Blueberry hill : Don't leave me now : Have I told you lately that I love you : I need you so

1958 : KING CREOLE (from the original soundtrack) SF 8231e
King Creole : As long as I have you : Hard headed woman : Trouble : Dixieland rock : Don't ask me why : Lover doll : Crawfish : Young dreams : Steadfast, loyal and true : New Orleans

1958 : ELVIS' GOLDEN RECORDS – VOL. 1 SF 8129
Hound dog : I love you because : All shook up : Heartbreak Hotel : You're a heartbreaker : Love me : Too much : Don't be cruel : That's when your heartaches begin : I'll never let you go : Love me tender : I forgot to remember to forget : Anyway you want me (that's how I will be) : I want you, I need you, I love you

1959 : ELVIS PK 11529
That's all right : Lawdy, Miss Clawdy : Mystery train : Playing for keeps : Poor boy : Money honey : I'm counting on you : My baby left me : I was the one : Shake, rattle and roll : I'm left, you're right, she's gone : You're a heartbreaker : Tryin' to get to you : Blue suede shoes

1959 : ELVIS' GOLDEN RECORDS – VOL. 2 SF 8151
I need your love tonight : Don't : Wear my ring around your neck : My wish came true : I got stung : Loving you : (Let me be your) Teddy bear : One night : A big hunk o' love : I beg you : A fool such as I : Doncha' think it's time : Jailhouse rock : Treat me nice

1960 : ELVIS IS BACK SF 5060
Make me know it : Fever : The girl of my best friend : I will be home again : Dirty, dirty feeling : The thrill of your love : Soldier boy : Such a night : It feels so right : The girl next door : Like a baby : Reconsider baby

1960 : G.I. BLUES (from the original soundtrack) SF 5078
Tonight is so right for love : What's she really like : Frankfort special : Wooden heart : G.I. blues : Pocketful of rainbows : Shoppin' around : Big boots : Didja' ever : Blue suede shoes : Doin' the best I can

1961 : BLUE HAWAII (from the original soundtrack) SF 8145
Blue Hawaii : Almost always true : Aloha-oe : No more : Can't help falling in love : Rock-a-hula baby : Moonlight swim : Ku-u-i-po (Hawaiian sweetheart) : Ito eats : Slicin' sand : Hawaiian sunset : Beach boy blues : Island of love : Hawaiian wedding song

1961 : HIS HAND IN MINE SF 8207
His hand in mine : I'm gonna walk dem golden stairs : In my Father's house : Milky white way : Known only to Him : I believe in the man in the sky : Joshua fit the battle : Jesus knows what I need : Swing down sweet chariot : Mansion over the hilltop : If we never meet again : Working on the building

1961 : SOMETHING FOR EVERYBODY SF 5106
There's always me : Give me the right : It's a sin : Sentimental me : Starting today : Gently : I'm coming home : In your arms : Put the blame on me : Judy : I want you with me : I slipped, I stumbled, I fell

1962 : GIRLS ! GIRLS ! GIRLS ! PL 42354
Girls, girls, girls : I don't want to be tied : Where do you come from : I don't want to : We'll be together : A boy like me, a girl like you : Earth boy : Return to sender : Because of love : Thanks to the rolling sea : Song of the shrimp : Walls have ears : We're coming in loaded

1963 : FUN IN ACAPULCO PL 42357
Fun in Acapulco : Vino, dinero y amor : Mexico : El Toro : Marguerita : The bullfighter was a lady : No room to rhumba : I think I'm gonna like it here : Bossa nova baby : You can't say no in Acapulco : Guadalajara : Love me tonight : Slowly but surely

1963 : ELVIS' GOLDEN RECORDS – VOL. 3 SF 7630
It's now or never : Stuck on you : Fame and fortune : I gotta know : Surrender : I feel so bad : Are you lonesome tonight : His latest flame : Little sister : Good luck charm : Anything that's part of you : She's not you

1964 : KISSIN' COUSINS PL 42355
Kissin' cousins (no. 2) : Smokey mountain boy : There's gold in the mountains : One boy, two little girls : Catchin' on fast : Tender fell feeling : Anyone : Barefoot ballad : Once is enough : Kissin' cousins : Echoes of love : Long lonely highway

1964 : ROUSTABOUT PL 42366
Roustabout : Little Egypt : Poison ivy league : Hard knocks : Its a wonderful world : Big love, big heartache : One-track heart : It's carnival time : Carny town : There's a brand new day on the horizon

1966 : HOW GREAT THOU ART SF 8206
How great Thou art : In the garden : Somebody bigger than you and I : Farther along : Stand by me : Without Him : So high : Where could I go but to the Lord : By and by : If the Lord wasn't walking by my side : Run on : Where no one stands alone : Crying in the chapel

1968: ELVIS' GOLDEN RECORDS – VOL. 4 SF 7924
Love letters & Witchcraft & It hurts me : What'd I say : Please don't drag that string around : Indescribably blue : You're the devil in disguise & Lonely man & A mess of blues & Ask me : Ain't that loving you baby : Just tell her Jim said hello

1969 : FROM ELVIS IN MEMPHIS SF 8029
Wearin' that loved on look : Only the strong survive : I'll hold you in my heart : Long black limousine : It keeps right on a-hurtin' : I'm moving on : Power of my love : Gentle on my mind : After loving you : True love travels on a gravel road : Any day now : In the ghetto

1970 : FROM MEMPHIS TO VEGAS SF 80801-1
Elvis at the International Hotel, Las Vegas
Blue suede shoes : Johnny B. Goode & All shook up & Are you lonesome tonight : Hound dog : I can't stop loving you : My babe : Medley – Mystery train – Tiger man : Words & In the ghetto & Suspicious minds & Can't help falling in love
FROM VEGAS TO MEMPHIS
Elvis back in Memphis
Inherit the wind : This is the story : Stranger in my own home town : A little bit of green : And the grass won't pay no mind : Do you know who I am : From a Jack to a King : The fair's moving on : You'll think of me : Without love
(2 records in special folder sleeve with colour photo insert)

1970 : THAT'S THE WAY IT IS SF 8162
I just can't help believin' : Twenty days and twenty nights : How the web was woven : Patch it up : Mary in the morning : You don't have to say you love me : You've lost that lovin' feelin' & I've lost you : Just pretend : Stranger in the crowd : The next step is love : Bridge over troubled water

1970 : ON STAGE FEBRUARY 1970 SF 8128
Elvis at the International Hotel, Las Vegas
See see rider blues : Release me (and let me love again) : Sweet Caroline : Runaway : The wonder of you : Polk salad Annie : Yesterday : Proud Mary : Walk a mile in my shoes : Let it be me

1970 : WORLD WIDE 50 GOLD AWARD HITS – VOL. 1 LPM 6401
Heartbreak Hotel : I was the one : I want you, I need you, I love you : Don't be cruel : Hound dog : Love me tender : Anyway you want me : Too much : Playing for keeps : All shook up : That's when your heartaches begin : Loving you : Teddy bear : Jailhouse rock : Treat me nice : I beg of you : Don't : Wear my ring around your neck : Hard headed woman : I got stung : A fool such as I : A big hunk o' love : Stuck on you : A mess of blues : It's now or never : I gotta know : Are you lonesome tonight : Surrender : I feel so bad : Little sister : Can't help falling in love : Rock-a-hula baby : Anything that's part of you : Good luck charm : She's not you : Return to sender : Where do you come from ? : One broken heart for sale : You're the devil in disguise : Bossa nova baby : Kissin' cousins : Viva Las Vegas : Ain't that loving you baby : Wooden heart : Crying in the chapel : If I can dream : In the ghetto : Suspicious minds : Don't cry daddy : Kentucky rain : Excerpt from a Press interview with Elvis at the time of his sailing in the U.S.S. Randall
(4 records in box with photograph album)

1971 : I'M 10,000 YEARS OLD, ELVIS COUNTRY SF 8172
Snowbird & Tomorrow never comes : Little cabin on the hill : Whole lot-ta shakin' goin' on : Funny how time slips away : I really don't want to know & There goes my everything : It's your baby, you rock it : The fool : Faded love : I washed my hands in muddy water : Make the world go away

1971 : WORLD WIDE 50 GOLD AWARD HITS – VOL. 2 : THE OTHER SIDES LPM 6402
Puppet on a string : Witchcraft : Trouble : Poor boy : I want to be free : Don'cha think it's time : Young dreams : The next step is love : You don't have to say you love me : Paralyzed : My wish came true : When my blue moon turns to gold again : Lonesome cowboy : My baby left me : It hurts me : I need your love tonight : Tell me why : Please don't drag that string around : Young and beautiful : Hot dog : New Orleans : We're gonna move : Crawfish : King Creole : I believe in the man in the sky : Dixieland rock : The wonder of you : They remind me too much of you : Mean woman blues : Lonely man : Any day now : Don't ask me why : His latest flame : I really don't want to know : Baby I don't care : I've lost you : Let me : Love me : Got a lot o' livin' to do : Fame and fortune : Rip it up : There goes my everything : Lover doll : One night : Just tell her Jim said hello : Ask me : Patch it up : As long as I have you : You'll think of me : Wild in the country
(4 records in box)

1972 : ELVIS NOW SF 8266
Help me make it through the night & Miracle of the rosary : Hey Jude : Put your hand in the hand & Until it's time for you to go & We can make the morning : Early mornin' rain : Sylvia : Fools rush in (where angels fear to tread) : I was born about ten thousand years ago

1972 : ELVIS LIVE AT MADISON SQUARE GARDEN SF 8296
Introduction : Theme from "2001 – A Space Odyssey" : That's all right : Proud Mary : Never been to Spain : You don't have to say you love me : You've lost that lovin' feelin' : Polk salad Annie : Love me : All shook up : Heartbreak Hotel : Medley : (Let me be your) Teddy bear – Don't be cruel – Love me tender : The impossible dream : Introductions by Elvis : Hound dog : Suspicious minds : For the good times : American trilogy : Funny how time slips away : I can't stop loving you : Can't help falling in love

1973 : ALOHA FROM HAWAII VIA SATELLITE DPS 2040
Theme from "2001 – A Space Odyssey" : See see rider : Burning love : Something : You gave me a mountain : Steamroller blues : My way : Love me : Johnny B. Goode : It's over : Blue suede shoes : I'm so lonesome I could cry : I can't stop loving you : Hound dog : What now my love : Fever : Welcome to my world : Suspicious minds : I'll remember you : Medley – Long tall Sally/Whole lotta shakin' goin' on : American trilogy : A big hunk o' love : Can't help falling in love

1973 : HITS OF THE 70s LPL1 7527
The wonder of you : I'm leavin' : Burning love : Always on my mind : I just can't help believing : You don't have to say you love me : There goes my everything : Rags to riches : Until it's time for you to go : Kentucky rain : I've lost you : An American trilogy

1974 : ELVIS – A LEGENDARY PERFORMER – VOL. 1 CPL1 0341
That's all right : I love you because : Heartbreak Hotel : Elvis (excerpt from an interview held September 22, 1958) : Don't be cruel : Love me : Trying to get to you : Love me tender : (There'll be) Peace in the valley (for me) : Elvis (further excerpt from an interview held September 22, 1958) : A fool such as I : Tonight is so right for love : Are you lonesome tonight : Can't help falling in love

1974 : GOOD TIMES APL1 0475
Take good care of her : Loving arms : I got a feelin' in my body : If that isn't love : She wears my ring : I've got a thing about you baby : My boy : Spanish eyes : Talk about the good times : Good Time Charlie's got the blues

1974 : ELVIS AS RECORDED LIVE ON STAGE IN MEMPHIS APL1 0606
See see rider : I got a woman : Love me : Trying to get to you : Medley – Long tall Sally/Whole lot-ta shakin' goin' on/Mama don't dance/Flip, flop and fly/Jailhouse rock/Hound dog : Why me, Lord : How great Thou art : Medley – Blueberry Hill/I can't stop loving you : Help me : An American trilogy : Let me be there : My baby left me : Lawdy, Miss Clawdy : Can't help falling in love

1975 : PROMISED LAND APL1 0873
Promised land : There's a honky tonk angel (who will take me back in) : Help me : Mr. Songman : Love song of the year & It's midnight & Your love's been a long time coming : If you talk in your sleep : Thinking about you & You ask me to

1975 : PICTURES OF ELVIS HY 1023
Return to sender : Roustabout : Little Egypt : Paradise Hawaiian style : Girls, girls, girls : Double trouble : Do the clam : Fun in Acapulco : Bossa nova baby : Clambake : Girl happy : Rock-a-hula baby

1975 : TODAY RS 1011
T-r-o-u-b-l-e : And I love you so : Susan when she tried : Woman without love : Shake a hand : Pieces of my life : Fairytale : I can help : Bringing it back : Green, green grass of home

1976 : THE ELVIS PRESLEY SUN COLLECTION HY 1001
That's all right mama : Blue moon of Kentucky : I don't care if the sun don't shine : Good rockin' tonight : Milk cow blues boogie : You're a heartbreaker : I'm left, you're right, she's gone : Baby let's play house : Mystery train : I forgot to remember to forget : I'll never let you go : I love you because (1st version) : Tryin' to get to you : Blue moon : Just because : I love you because (2nd version)
Recorded 1954–1955

1976 : ELVIS – A LEGENDARY PERFORMER – VOL. 2 CPL1 1349
Harbour lights : Interview with Elvis by Jay Thompson backstage following a live performance in Wichita Falls, Texas : I want you, I need you, I love you : Blue suede shoes : Blue Christmas : Jailhouse rock : It's now or never : Cane and a high starched collar : Presentation of awards to Elvis (excerpt from press conference, Pearl Harbor, Hawaii, March 25th 1961) : Blue Hawaii : Such a night : Baby what you want me to do : How great Thou art : If I can dream

1976 : FROM ELVIS PRESLEY BOULEVARD, MEMPHIS, TENNESSEE RS 1060
Hurt : Never again : Blue eyes crying in the rain : Danny Boy : The last farewell : For the heart : Bitter they are, harder they fall : Solitaire : Love coming down : I'll never fall in love again

1977 : ELVIS IN DEMAND PL 42003
Suspicion : Hi heel sneakers : Got a lot o' livin' to do : Have I told you lately that I love you ? : Please don't drag that string around : It's only love : The sound of your cry : Viva Las Vegas : Do not disturb : Tomorrow is a long time : It's a long lonely highway : Puppet on a string : The first time ever I saw her face : Summer kisses and winter tears : It hurts me : Let it be me

1977 : WELCOME TO MY WORLD PL 12274
Welcome to my world : Help me make it through the night : Release me (and let me love again) : I really don't want to know : For the good times : Make the world go away : Gentle on my mind : I'm so lonesome I could cry : Your cheatin' heart : I can't stop loving you

1977 : MOODY BLUE PL 12428
Unchained melody : If you love me (let me know) : Little Darlin' : He'll have to go : Let me be there : Way down : Pledging my love : Moody blue : She thinks I still care : It's easy for you

1977 : ELVIS IN CONCERT (double album) PL 22587
CC rider : That's all right : Are you lonesome tonight : Teddy bear : Don't be cruel : You gave me a mountain : How great Thou art : I really don't want to know : Hurt : Hound dog : My way : Can't help falling in love : I gotta woman amen : Love me : If you love me let me know : O sole mio/It's now or never : Tryin' to get to you : Hawaiian wedding song : Fairy tale : Little sister : Early morning rain : What'd I say : Johnny B. Goode : And I love you so

A BIG HUNK OF LOVE

Words and Music by Sid Wyche
and Aaron Schroeder

G (tacet)
1. Don't be a stin-gy lit-tle ma-ma;
nat-'ral born bee-hive,
G (tacet)
You 'bout to starve me half to death.
Filled _ with hon - ey to the top.
G (tacet)
Now you could spare a kiss or two and still have plen-ty left.
But I ain't greed-y, ba-by, all I want is all you got.
Oh, no, no,
C7
ba - by.
I ain't ask- in' much of
G
you.
Just a
D7
Db7
C7
G
1
2
big-a big-a big-a hunk o' love will do.
2. You're just a

G (tacet) G (tacet)
3. I got a wish-bone in my pock-et. I got a rab-bit's foot 'round my wrist. And I'd have
G (tacet) G (tacet) G (tacet) G (tacet)
ev - 'ry-thing my luck-y charms could bring if you gim-me just one sweet
G (tacet) C7 G
kiss, oh, no no no no no no, ba - by. I ain't ask-in' much of you.
D7 Db7 C7 G C7 G
Just a big-a big-a big-a hunk o' love will do.

ALL SHOOK UP

Words and Music by
Otis Blackwell and Elvis Presley

Medium Shuffle Rhythm

hands are sha - ky and my knees are weak, I can't seem to stand on my
Bb
own two feet, Who do you thank when you have such luck? I'm in love! I'm
All Shook Up! Mm mm, oh, oh, yeah, yeah!
Eb7
F7
Bb
Eb7
Bb
1. Please don't ask what's on my mind, I'm a lit-tle mixed up but I'm feel - in' fine When I'm
2. Tongue get's tied when I try to speak, My in - side shakes like a leaf on a tree, There's
Eb7
Bb
near that girl that I love best, My heart beats so it scares me to death!
on-ly one cure for this soul of mine, That's to have the girl that I love so fine! She
Opt
Eb7
F7

touched my hand, What a chill I got, Her kiss - es are like a vol -
Bb
- ca - no that's hot! I'm proud to say she's my but - ter cup, I'm in love! I'm
1
All Shock Up! Mm mm oh, oh, yeah, - yeah! 2 My
Eb7
F7
Bb
Eb7
Bb
2
yeah! I'm All Shook Up! Mm mm oh, oh, yeah, yeah! I'm
Bb
Eb7
F7
Bb
All Shook Up! Mm mm oh, oh, yeah, yeah! I'm All Shook Up!
Eb7
F7
Bb

AIN'T THAT LOVING YOU BABY

Words and Music by
Clyde Otis and Ivory Joe Hunter

C7
Ain't that lov - in' you, ba - by? Ain't that
G7
F7
lov - in' you, ba - by, Ain't that lov - in' you so?
1. 2. 3.
C7
F7
4.
C7
2. I could
3. If you
4. I'm put - tin'
F7
G7
Ain't that lov - in' you, ba - by,
F7
C (Tacet)
Ain't that lov - in' you so?

A MESS OF BLUES

Words and Music by
Doc Pomus and Mort Shuman

G7
F7
C
gone I got a mess of blues.
gone I got a mess of blues.
1. G7
2. C7
F7
I ain't
Whoops, there goes a tear - drop,
C
B7
C7
F7
roll - in' down my face.
If you cry when
F7
G7 (tacet)
you're in love, it sure ain't no dis-grace.
I got - ta

C
get my - self to - geth- er be - fore I lose my
C
F7
mind. I'm gon - na catch the next train go-in' and
F7
G7
leave my blues be - hind. Since you're gone I
F7
C
1. Ab7
G7
2. C F7 C
got a mess of blues. I just.

ANYTHING THAT'S PART OF YOU

Words and Music by
Don Robertson

E♭ (tacet)
I kept a rib-bon from your hair;
E♭
E♭maj.7
E♭7
A breath of per-fume lin-gers
A♭
there.
It helps to cheer me when I'm blue,
E♭ (B♭7) E♭
B♭
An-y-thing that's part of you.
E♭
A♭
B♭ (tacet)
Oh, how it hurts to miss you
A♭
so when I know
B♭7
Fm7
E♭
you don't love me an-y-

A♭
E♭
more, To go on need-ing you, know-ing you don't need
B♭ B♭7 B♭6 B♭7 (Tacet)
E♭ E♭maj.7
me. No rea-son left for me to live.
E♭7
A♭
What can I take, what can I give, When I'd give all of some-one
E♭ (B♭7) E♭
B♭
B♭7
1. E♭ A♭
new For an-y-thing that's part of you.
E♭ (tacet)
2. E♭ A♭ E♭
I mem-o-rize the notes you you.
rall.
Ped.

ANYWAY YOU WANT ME

Words and Music by
Aaron Schroeder and Cliff Owens

that's how I will be.
In your hands my heart is clay, to
take and mould as you may.
I'm what you make me; you've on-ly to take me, and
in your arms I will stay.
I'll be a fool or a wise man; my
dar-ling, you hold the key.
Yes, an-y-way you want me, well,
that's how I will be.
be, I will be.
Bb
F7
Eb
C7
Gm
Bb7
Edim7
ff
mp
mf
rit.
1
2

ARE YOU LONESOME TONIGHT?

Words and Music by
Roy Turk and Lou Handman

RECITATION

I wonder if you're lonesome to-night?
You know, someone said "The world's a stage, and each must play a part"
Fate had me playing 'in love' with you as my sweetheart,
Act one was where we met; I loved you at first glance.

You read your lines so cleverly, and never missed a cue
Then came act two.
You seemed to change, you acted strange, and why? I'll never know.

Honey, you lied when you said "You loved me" and I had no cause to doubt you
But I'd rather go on hearing your lies than to go on living without you.
Now the stage is bare, and I'm standing there with emptiness all around
And if you won't come back to me, then they can ring the curtain down.

At end of Recitation ⊕, sing, "Is your heart" etc

BABY LET'S PLAY HOUSE

Words and Music by
Arthur Gunter

2. Now, listen and I'll tell you, baby,
What I'm talkin' about.
Come on back to me, little girl,
So we can play some house, now baby,

(TO CHORUS)

3. Now, this is one thing, baby,
That I want you to know,
Come on back and let's play a little house
So we can act like we did before, now baby,

(TO CHORUS)

4. Now, listen to me baby,
Try to understand,
I'd rather see you dead, little girl,
Than to be with another man. Now, baby,

(TO CHORUS)

BLUE CHRISTMAS

Words and Music by
Billy Hayes and Jay Johnson

With expression

F C7

I'll have a BLUE CHRIST-MAS with - out you ___ I'll be so

F Cm6 D7

blue think - ing a - bout you ___ Dec - o - ra - tions of

Cm6 D7 Gm G7

red on a green Christ-mas tree Won't mean a thing if

C7
F
C7
you're not here with me. I'll have a BLUE CHRIST-MAS, that's cer-tain
F
And when that blue heart-ache starts hurt-in' You'll be
Cm6
D7
Cm6
D7
Gm
Fdim
C7
do-in' all right, with your Christ-mas of white, But I'll have a
1
2
F
F
blue, BLUE CHRIST-MAS I'll have a CHRIST-MAS
rit

BLUE SUEDE SHOES

Words and Music by
Carl Lee Perkins

knock me down, step in my face, slan-der my name all o-ver the place;
Burn my house, steal my car, drink my li-quor from my old-fruit jar;
Tacet F Tacet F Tacet F
Do an-y-thing that you want to do, but uh-uh, hon-ey lay off of my shoes
Tacet F Tacet
Don't you step on my Blue Suede Shoes. You can do an-y-thing but lay
Bb F C7
off of my Blue Suede Shoes.
Shoes.
1
2
C7sus4 F Bb7 F Tacet F Bb7 F

BURNING LOVE

Words and Music by
Dennis Linde

Verse 3

I'm coming closer, the flames are now lickin' my body;
Won't you help me, I feel like I'm slippin' away;
It's hard to breathe and my chest is a-heavin';
Lord have mercy, I'm burnin' a hole where I lay; (REPEAT CHORUS & FADE)

CAN'T HELP FALLING IN LOVE

Words and Music by
George Weiss, Hugo Peretti and Luigi Creatore

help fall-ing in love with you. Like a riv-er flows
Cm Fm Eb Bb7 Eb Gm Am D7
sure-ly to the sea Dar-ling so it goes some things are meant to be
Gm Am D7 Gm Am D7 Gm C7 Fm7 Bb7
Take my hand, take my whole life too For
Eb Gm Cm Ab Eb Bb7
I can't help fall-ing in love with you.
Ab Bb7 Cm Fm Eb Bb7 Eb

CRYING IN THE CHAPEL

Words and Music by
Arthur Glenn

I pray the Lord that I'll grow strong - er, As I live from day to day.
You'll know the mean - ing of con - tent - ment, Then you'll be hap-py with the Lord.
I've searched and I've searched, but I could - n't find No way on earth to gain peace of
You'll search and you'll search, but you'll nev - er find No way on earth to gain peace of
mind. Now I'm hap - py in the chap - el, Where peo-ple are of one ac - cord;
mind. Take your trou - bles to the chap - el, Get down on your knees and pray;
We gath - er in the chap - el, Just to sing and praise the
Your bur - dens will be light - er, And you'll sure - ly find the
1.
Lord.
mf
2. Ev - 'ry sin - ner looks for
2.
way.
mf

(YOU'RE SO SQUARE) BABY I DON'T CARE

Words and Music by
Jerry Leiber and Mike Stoller

G7
C
F
C
C
F
You don't like hot rod rac - in' or driv- in' late at night.
C
C
F
C
F
You just wan - na park where it's nice and dark; you
C
F
C
C7
F7
G7 (Tacet)
just wan- na hold me tight. You're so square,
But, ba - by, I don't
C
C7
F
F#dim7
care. You don't know an - y dance steps that are

C
C7
F
F♯dim7
G7
new,
But
no one else can
love me like you
do.
I don't know why my heart - flips;
I on - ly know it does. —
I
C F C C F C
won - der why I love you, babe, I guess it's just be - cause you're so square, —
C F C F C C C7 F
G7 (Tacet)
1. C F7 G7 (Tacet)
2. C F7 C
And, ba - by, I don't care.
You
care. —

DON'T

Words and Music by
Jerry Leiber and Mike Stoller

1
F
Dm
Gm7
C7
2
F
F7
don't.
don't.
Bb
A
A7
Bb
C7
F
Bb
F
If you think that this is just a game I'm play - ing,
G7
C7
Bdim7
If you think that I don't mean ev - 'ry word I'm
C7
F
C7
say - ing,
Don't,
(don't)
don't
(don't)

F F7 Bb C7 F Am Dm
3
don't feel that way. I'm your love and yours I will
3
3
Gm7 C7 (tacet) F F7
stay. This you can be - lieve; I will nev - er
Bb Gm7 C7 F Dm Gm7 sus4 C7 C7
leave you, Heav-en knows I won't. Ba - by, don't say
1 F Bb7 F C7
don't.
2 F Bb7 F
don't.

DON'T CRY DADDY

Words and Music by
Scott Davis

F♯
G
—— in - side my cof - fee cup, kept cry-ing but —— and ring - ing in my
—— my lit - tle chil - dren so, I won - der — will it be — the — same to -
C
A
Chorus
D
ears. ——
night. ——
Don't cry Dad - dy, ——
mf
Em
A
Dad-dy, please don't cry; ——
Dad - dy,
G
A
D
G
you've still got me and lit - tle Tom - my, To - geth-er we'll find a brand — new mom-my,

D
A7
Dad-dy, Dad - dy, please laugh a - gain,
Dad-dy, ride us on your back a - gain, Oh,
G F♯m Em A7
D
1.
F (D)
G (D)
Dad - dy, please don't cry.
D
C (D)
D
C (D)
2.
F (D)
G F♯m Em
A7
D
Oh, Dad - dy, please don't cry.

DON'T LEAVE ME NOW

Words and Music by
Aaron Schroeder and Ben Weisman

C7
F
G7
This heart that loves you. There'd just be nŏth-in' for me
If you should leave me now.
C
F7
C
(Tacet)
What good is
F
dream - ing if I must dream all a - lone by my-
C
F7
C
(Tacet)
D7
self? With-out you, dar - lin', My dreams would just gath-er
mf

G7 (Tacet)
dust like a book on a shelf. Come fill these arms,
mp
C
C7
F
That long to hold you. Don't close your
G7
(Tacet)
1. C
Ab7
eyes to my plea. Oh, don't you leave me now!
G7 (Tacet)
2. C
F7
C
Don't leave me now, now!
mp
ff

(YOU'RE THE) DEVIL IN DISGUISE

Words and Music by
Bill Giant, Bernie Baum and Florence Kaye

Dm
F
1.You fooled me with your kiss - es,
2. I thought that I was in heav - en,
Dm
You cheat - ed and you schemed,
But I was sure sur - prised,
F
Heav - en knows how you
Heav - en help me, I
Dm
lied to me,
did - n't see
B♭
C7
F
You're not the way you seemed.
the dev - il in your eyes.
You
Coda
Dm
Dev - il in dis - guise,
F
Oh, yes, you are.
Dm
Dev - il in dis -
Repeat - ad lib. - fading out

DON'T BE CRUEL

Words and Music by
Otis Blackwell and Elvis Presley

Medium bright (with good beat)

Don't stop thinking of me, Don't make me feel this way, Come on o-ver here and love me, You
walk up to the preacher, and let us say "I do." Then you'll know you have me, And I'll
C
C7
F
know what I want you to say. Don't Be Cruel to a heart that's true. Why
know I'll have you too. Don't Be Cruel to a heart that's true. I don't
C
Dm7
G7
C
1
should we be a-part? I real-ly love you, ba-by, cross my heart. Let's
want no oth-er love, Ba-by, it's just you I'm think-ing
F
2
G7
F
G7
C
of. Don't Be Cruel to a heart that's true. Don't Be Cruel to a heart that's
C
Dm7
G7
C
Dm7
G7
true. I don't want no oth-er love Ba-by, it's just you I'm thinking of.
C
C7
F
G7
F
G7
C

THE GIRL OF MY BEST FRIEND

Words and Music by
Beverly Ross and Sam Bobrick

Her love-ly hair,
Her skin so fair,
F
Dm
C7
F
Dm
C7
I could go on 'n ne-ver end.
Oh, I can't
F
Dm
C
B♭
help it I'm in love
With the girl of my best
C
F
Dm
B♭
Gm
friend.
I want to tell her how I love her
F
F7
E♭
C7
F

so, And hold her in my arms, but then
Dm Gm7 C7 F F7
What if she got real mad and told him so, I could ne-ver face
Bb C7 F Dm G7
ei-ther one a-gain. (Uh huh huh) The way they kiss,
C7 F Dm C7
Their hap-pi-ness; Will my ache-in' heart e-ver mend
F Dm C7 F Dm C

Or will I al-ways be in love With the
B♭ C F Dm
Girl of My Best Friend?
B♭ Gm F Dm C7
Ne - ver end, will it e - ver
Dm C7 F Dm C7 F
end Please let it end.
Dm C7 F Dm C7 F

GOT A LOT OF LIVIN' TO DO

Featured by Elvis Presley in the Paramount Film 'Loving You'

Words and Music by
Aaron Schroeder and Ben Weisman

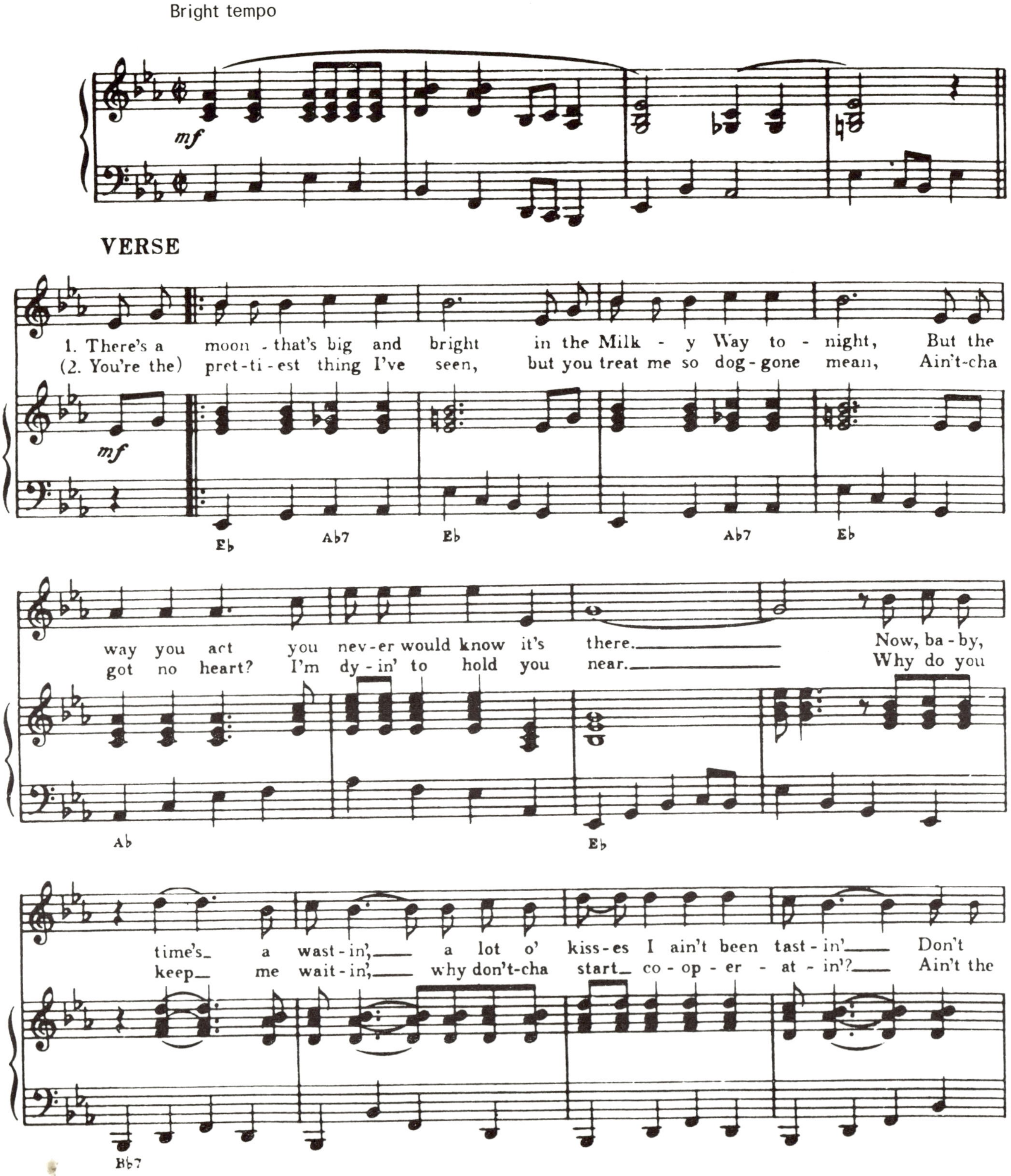

mf

VERSE

1. There's a moon - that's big and bright in the Milk - y Way to - night, But the
(2. You're the) pret - ti - est thing I've seen, but you treat me so dog - gone mean, Ain't-cha

mf

Eb Ab7 Eb Eb Ab7 Eb

way you act you nev - er would know it's there. Now, ba - by,
got no heart? I'm dy - in' to hold you near. Why do you

Ab Eb

time's a wast - in', a lot o' kiss - es I ain't been tast - in' Don't
keep me wait - in', why don't-cha start co - op - er - at - in'? Ain't the

Bb7

know a-bout you but I'm a-gon-na get my share. Oh, yes, I've
things I say the things you wan-na hear?
Ab
Bb7
Eb
(Tacet)
CHORUS
Spoken
Got a lot o' liv-in' to do, Whole lot o' lov-in' to do. Come on,
Bb7
Eb
ba-by! To make it fun it takes two. Oh, yes, I've got a lot o'
Ab7
Eb
(Tacet)
Bb7
liv-in' to do, Whole lot o' lov-in' to do, And there's no one who I'd rath-er
Eb
Ab
1
2
do it with-a than you! 2. You're the you!
Eb
Ab7
Eb
Eb
Ab7
Eb

HARD HEADED WOMAN

From the Paramount Motion Picture Production 'King Creole'

Words and Music by
Claude De Metruis

1
2
thorn in the side of man.
2. Now man.
Eb7
Bb
Gb7 F7
Bb
Gb7 F7
CHORUS
3. Now Sam-son told De - li - lah loud and clear Keep your cot - ton pick - in' fin-gers
4. (I) heard 'bout a king who was do - in' swell Till he start-ed play - in' with that
5. — I got a wom-an a head like a rock If she ev - er went a - way I'd
f
(Tacet)
(Tacet)
(Tacet)
Bb
Bb
Bb
out my curl - y hair
e - vil Jez - e - bel
cry a - round the clock
Oh, yeah, Ev-er since the world be - gan. Uh-huh-huh, A
Eb7
Bb
1-2
3
Hard Head-ed Wom-an been a thorn in the side of man.
4. I
5. –
man.
F7
Eb7
Bb
Gb7 F7
Bb Eb7
Bb

HEARTBREAK HOTEL

Words and Music by

Mae Boren Axton, Tommy Durden and Elvis Presley

C7
C
C7
still finds some room for bro-ken heart-ed lov-ers to cry there in the gloom and be so
F7
C
F7
C
lone-ly, oh so lone-ly, oh so lone-ly they could die! The
C
C 7
C
bell-hop's tears keep flow-ing the desk clerk's dressed in black, they've been so long on lone-ly street they
if your ba-by leaves and you have a tale to tell, just take a walk down lone-ly street to
C7
F7
C
nev-er will go back and they're so lone-ly oh they're so lone-ly They're so
Heart Break Ho-tel where you'll be lone-ly and I'll be lone-ly, we'll be so
F7
1. C
2. C
lone-ly they pray to die. So die.
lone-ly that we could
rit.

HOUND DOG

Words and Music by
Jerry Leiber and Mike Stoller

(tacet)
Bb
When they said you was high-classed, well, that was just a lie.
Eb7
Bb
When they said you was high-classed, well, that was just a lie.
F7
Eb7
Well, you ain't nev-er caught a rab-bit and you ain't no friend of
1
Bb
(tacet)
mine. You ain't noth-in' but a
2
Bb
Eb7
Bb
mine.

FEEL SO BAD

Words and Music by Chuck Willis

Shake my head and walk a - way.
Tacet
C
CHORUS
oo - oo - hu - oo - hu, peo - ple, that's the way I feel,
C
oo oo hu oo hu, peo - ple, that's the way I feel.
C7
F9
Some - times I think I won't, then a - gain I think I
G7
Tacet

To Coda
(VERSE 2)
will.
Some-times I want to stay here, then a-gain I want to
C
C
leave;
Some-times I want to leave here, then a-gain I want to
C7
F9
stay.
Yes, I've got my train fare pack my bag and ride a -
C
G7
D. S. al Coda
CODA
Tacet *
way.
C
C9 Db9 C13

HIS LATEST FLAME

Words and Music by
Doc Pomus and Mort Shuman

F
Dm
F
1.Dm (Tacet)
flame.
He talked and
2.Dm
C7
Bb
C7
Though I smiled, the tears in - side were a - burn - in'.
Bb
C7
Bb
C7
I wished him luck and then he said good - bye.
Bb
C7
Bb
C7
He was gone but still his words kept re - turn - in'.
Bb
C7
Bb
F
What else was there for me to do but cry.

Dm
F
Dm (Tacet)
F
Would you be - lieve
Dm
F
Dm
F
that yes - ter - day
This girl was in my arms and
Dm
F
Dm
swore to me
She'd be mine e - ter - nal - ly.
And Ma - rie's the
B♭
C7
1. F
Dm
F
name of his lat - est flame.
Dm (Tacet)
2. F
B♭7
F
B♭7
F
A ver - y old flame.

I BEG OF YOU

Words and Music by
Rose Marie McCoy and Kelly Owens

G7
F7
C
1
please don't break my heart, I beg of you. I don't
please don't say good - bye, I beg of you.
2
C7
F7
Hold my hand and prom-ise that you'll
C
F7
al - ways love me true. Make me know you
D7 (tacet)
sus4
G7
love me the same way I love you, lit-tle girl. You

C
got me at your mer-cy now that I'm in love with
C7
F7
you. So please don't take ad - van-tage 'cause you
C
G7
F7
C
know my love is true My dar-ling, please please love me too, I beg of you.
1
Ab7
G7
I don't
2
F7
C

I GOT STUNG!

Words and Music by
Aaron Schroeder and David Hill

me. It — start-ed in my eyes, crept up to my head. F - lew to my heart till
-fore. Start-ed buzz-in' in my ear, buzz-in' in my brain. Got stung all o-ver but I
Eb
Ab7
Eb
1
I was stung dead
feel no pain
I'm done, uh-huh, I Got Stung! Mm,
Eb Tacet Bb7 Tacet Ab7 Tacet Eb
2
Now don't think I'm com - plain - in' I'm might - y pleased we
Eb7 Ab Eb Bb7
met 'cause you gimme just one lit-tle peck on the back of my neck and I break out in a
Eb Ab Bb7 Tacet

cold cold sweat. If I live to a hun-dred and two, I won't let
Bb7
Eb
no-bod-y sting me but you. I'll be buzz-zin' 'round your hive ev-'ry
Eb
Ab
-day at five, and I'm nev-er gon-na leave once I ar-rive 'cause I'm done, uh-
Ab7
Eb
Tacet
Bb7
Tacet
1
2
-huh, I Got Stung! Mm, Stung!
A7
Tacet
Eb
Ab7
Bb7
Tacet
Eb
Ab7
Eb

I GOTTA KNOW

Words and Music by
Paul Evans and Matt Williams

D7 (tacet) G C 1 G
go. I got-ta know, got-ta know, got-ta know.
no. I got-ta know, got-ta know, got-ta
2 G C D7 G
know. Oh, how much I need you! Have
C D7 G C D7
pit-y on this heart of mine. Well, if you need and
G Em A7 (tacet) D7
want me too, I'll be your one and on-ly till the end of time.
(ti - ime)

G
Saw the for-tune tell - er; had my for-tune read. She sent me to the doc - tor, who
G G7 C
Sent me straight to bed. He said I'm lone-some and I'm love-sick. I've
G D7
got my mind on lip - stick. Will you kiss a - way my cares and
D7 (tacet) G C 1 G D7 2 G
woe? I got-ta know, got-ta know, got-ta know. know.

IF I CAN DREAM

Words and Music by
W. Earl Brown

peace — and un-der-stand-ing some-time, Strong winds of pro-mise — that will blow a - way — the
C Am F G11 C Am
doubt — and fear, If I can dream — of a warm-er sun — where hope keeps shin-ing on ev-er-y-one, tell me
Dm7 G9 G7 C C7 F E7 Am
why — oh — why-oh — why won't that sun ap - pear?
C Am F Dm7 G7 C F C C7
We're lost in a cloud — with too much rain, — We're trapped in a world —
f
F F♯dim C C7 F F♯dim
that's troub-led with pain, — but as long as a man has the strength to dream, he can re -
C C7 F F♯dim C E7 Am

-deem his soul, — his life. — Deep in my heart — there's a trem-blin'
mf
D7 G11 G7 C Am
ques-tion. Still, I am sure — that the ans-wer's — gon-na come — some-how. Out there in the
F G11 C Am Dm7 G9
dark — there's a beck-on-ing can - dle, — and while I can think, — while I can talk, while I can
C F F#dim C Am
stand, while I can walk, while I can dream, — feel-in' my dream — come
cresc.
C Am F G11
true — right now. —
Tacet * C F C

I JUST CAN'T HELP BELIEVIN'

Words and Music by
Cynthia Weil and Barry Mann

And I just can't help be - liev - in' when she's
And I just can't help be - liev - in' when she's
Fmaj7
ly - ing close be - side me, And my heart beats with the rhy -
whis - per - in' her mag - ic, And her tears are shin - in' hon -
Cm
(F bass)
thm of her sighs.
ey sweet with love.
B♭
(F bass)
B♭m
(F bass)
F
B♭
(F bass)
This time the girl is gon - na stay,

F
B♭
(F bass)
F
B♭maj9
(F bass)
This time the girl is gon-na stay,
B♭maj9
(C bass)
NC
For more than just a day.
F
B♭maj9
(C bass)
1.
2.
I
For more than just a day.
F
Keep repeating and fade-out

I'VE LOST YOU

Words and Music by
Ken Howard and Alan Blaikley

Bb7
Eb
F7
bod-y's still as kind, I've Lost You on the jour-ney but I can't re-mem-ber where or when.
Bb
F (A Bass)
Gm
Gm (F Bass)
Who can tell when sum-mer turns to au - tumn and who can
Six o - clock the ba - by will be cry - ing, and you will
mp
Eb
Eb (D Bass)
Cm7
F7 (sus 4)
F7
Bb
F (A Bass)
point the mo-ment love grows cold?
stum - ble sleep-ing to the door.
Soft-ly, with-out pain the joy is
In the chill and sull-en grey of
3
Gm
Gm (F Bass)
Bb
Eb
Eb (D Bass)
Cm7
F7 (sus 4)
F7
o - ver tho' why it's gone we neith-er of us know.
morn - ing we play the parts that we have learned too well.
Oh, I've
Oh, I've
mf

Bb
Bb7
Lost You, yes I've Lost You I can't reach you an - y - more, We
Lost You, oh, I've Lost You though you won't ad - mit it's so, I've
Eb
1. F7
ought to talk it o - ver now, but rea - son can't stand in for feel - ing.
Lost You on the jour - ney, but I
2. F7
Bb
F
(A Bass)
can't re - mem - ber where or when.
mp
Gm
Dm
Eb
Bb
(D Bass)
F7
(sus 4)
F7
D.S. Lyric 1 and fade
Oh, I've
mf
D.S. and fade

IT HURTS ME

Words and Music by
Joy Byers and Charles E. Daniels

C
Em
Am
Em
C7
whole town is talk-ing, they're call-ing you a fool For
F
G7
C
C7
lis-t'ning to his same old lies; And when I
F
F♯dim
C
E7
Am
know I could be so true, If I had some-one like you, It
D7
G7
C
C7
F
G7
hurts me to see the way he makes you cry. You love him so much,

C E7 Am F G7 C C7
you're too blind to see, He's on-ly play-ing a game;
F F♯dim C E7 Am
But he's nev-er loved you And he nev-er will And
D7 G7
dar-ling, don't you know he'll nev-er change. Oh,
C Em Am Em C7
I know that he nev-er will set you free,

F
G7
C
C7
Be - cause_ he's just that kind of guy; But if you
F
F♯dim
C
E7
Am
ev - er tell him you're through, I'll be wait - ing for you,
C
Am
C
Am
Wait - ing to hold you so_ tight, Wait - ing to kiss you good - night, Yes
Dm7
G7
C
G9
Cmaj.7
G9
C
dar - ling, if I had some - one like you.
rall.

I'M LEFT, YOU'RE RIGHT, SHE'S GONE

Words and Music by
Stanley A. Kesler and William E. Taylor

F C7 C7 F B♭7 F7
broke the ties that bind, And I know that she nev-er cared for me. Well, I
home for two or three And I'll soon for-get her now I know.
B♭ F B♭ F F7 B♭
thought I knew just what she'd do. I guess I'm not so smart, You tried to tell me all a-long she'd
F C7 F C7 F F
on-ly break my heart. You're right, I'm left, she's gone. You're right, I'm
F B♭ F C7
left all a-lone. She's gone I know not where, But now I just don't
F C7 1. F B♭7 F 2. F B♭7 F
care for now I have fall-en for you. You're you.

I LOVE YOU BECAUSE

Words and Music by
Leon Payne

you. No mat - ter what the world may say a - bout me.
wide. No mat - ter what may be the style or sea - son.
C F C C7 F Cdim C
I know your love will al - ways see me through. I
I know your heart will al - ways be true. I
D7 G7
love you for the way you nev - er doubt me But most of all I
love you for a hun - dred thous - and reas - ons But most of all I
C C7 F C
1 2
love you 'cause you're you. 2. I
love you 'cause you're you.
G7 C F C C F C

I NEED YOUR LOVE TONIGHT

Words and Music by
Sid Wayne and Bix Reichner

F C7 F Bb F C7
need your love to-night. I've been wait-in' just for to-night to do some lov-in' and
F Bb F G7 (tacet)
hold you tight. Don't tell me, ba-by, you got-ta go; I got the hi-fi high and the
C7 (tacet) F C7 F
lights down low. Hey, now, hear what I say. Ooh-wow, you bet-ter stay. Pow-
F F7 Bb F C7 F 1 C7 (tacet) 2
pow, don't run a-way. I need your love to-night. Oh,

IT'S NOW OR NEVER

Words and Music by
G. Capurro and E. Di Capua
English Lyric by
Aaron Schroeder and Wally Gold

Eb
To Interlude
3.
Bb7
Eb
Fine
(opt. octave lower.................)
wait. 1. When I first my love won't wait.
Just like a
mp
INTERLUDE
Eb
Eb+
Ab
Bb7
saw you, with your smile so ten-der, My heart was cap-tured;
wil - low we would cry an o-cean, If we lost true love
Ab
Ebm Eb
(tacet)
Eb
Eb+
my soul sur - ren-dered. I've spent a life - time wait-ing for the
and sweet de - vo-tion. Your lips ex - cite me; let your arms in-
(Return to Chorus)
Ab
Abm
Eb
Fdim7 Fm7 Bb7
Eb Abm
Eb
right time. Now that you're near the time is here at last.
- vite me For who knows when we'll meet a-gain this way.
(Return To Chorus)

I WANT YOU, I NEED YOU, I LOVE YOU

Music by
Ira Kosloff
Words by
Maurice Mysels

love you — More and more. I thought I could live with-out ro-mance — Be-
-fore you came to me, But now I know that I will go on lov-ing you e-ter-nal-
-ly. Won't you please be my own Nev-er leave me a-lone, 'Cause I die ev-'ry time we're a-
-part. — I want you, I need you, I love you — With all my heart. Hold me heart.
A7 Dm7 G7 C Fm C Gm7 C7 F
Gm7 C7 sus4 C7 F Am7 D7 G Em Am7 D7
G7sus4 G7 C Am Dm G7 C C7
F C B7 A7 Dm7 G7 C A♭7 G7 Tacet C
1
2

JAILHOUSE ROCK

Words and Music by
Jerry Leiber and Mike Stoller

EXTRA CHORUSES

4. The sad sack was a-sittin' on a block of stone,
Way over in the corner weeping all alone.
The warden said, "Hey buddy, don't you be no square,
If you can't find a partner, use a wooden chair!"
Let's rock, etc.

5. Shifty Henry said to Bugs, "For Heaven's sake,
No one s lookin', now's our chance to make a break."
Bugsy turned to Shifty and he said, "Nix, nix,
I wanna stick around a while and get my kicks,"
Let's rock, etc.

KENTUCKY RAIN

Words and Music by
Eddie Rabbitt and Dick Heard

C
Am
D7
run - nin' to or from, All I know is I
mem - 'ry was-n't clear, Was it yes - ter - day, no
G7
want to bring you home. So I'm
wait, the day be - fore.
C
G
C
F
Walk - ing in the rain, thumb - ing for a ride, On this
Fi - n'ly got a ride with a preach-er man who asked, "Where you
C
F
C
C7
F
G
lone - ly Ken-tuck - y back road. I've loved you much too long and
bound on such a dark aft - er noon?" As we drove on thru the rain, as he

C Am D7
my love's too strong, To let you go, nev-er know-ing what went
lis-tened, I ex-plained, And he left me with a prayer that I'd find
G7 Fmaj7 D7
wrong.
you.
Ken-tuck-y rain keeps pour-ing
C Bm Em Am G F Em
down,
And up a-head's an-oth-er town that I'll go
F C Fmaj7 C Em
walk-ing thru,
With the rain in my shoes,

Am
Em
C
Am
Am7
F
3
Searching for you.
G7
C
Em
F
G7
In the cold Kentucky rain,
In the cold Kentucky
1.
C
rain.
12
8
4
4
2.
C
Em
F
rain,
In the cold Kentucky
Repeat till fade

KING CREOLE

From the Paramount Motion Picture Production 'King Creole'

Words and Music by
Jerry Leiber and Mike Stoller

F (Tacet)
He goes by the name of King Cre - ole.
He bends a string and "that's all she wrote."
He wails some blues a - bout New Or - leans.
He don't stop play - in' till the gui - tar breaks.
Chorus
(Tacet)
B♭7
You know he's gone, gone, gone, Jump - in' like a cat - fish on a
F
C7
pole. You know he's gone, gone,
B♭7
F
gone, Hip - shak - ing King Cre - ole.
1.2.3.
B♭7
C7 (Tacet)
4.
B♭7
F
2. When the
3. Well, he
4. Well, he

LAWDY MISS CLAWDY

Words and Music by
Lloyd Price

F
B♭
A
C
B♭
F
B♭6
Bdim
F
F6
3. I'm gon-na tell, tell my ma-ma. Lawd, I'm gon-na tell her what you been do-ing to me
4. Well now Law-dy, Law-dy, Law-dy Miss Claw-dy Girl! you sure look good to me
5. Well so bye, bye, bye, bye, ba-by Girl! I won't be trou-ble no more
C 7
F
F7
F
F6
F7
F6
F7
B♭
B6
B♭7
I'm gon-na tell ev-'ry-bo-dy that I'm down in mis-er-y
You just wheel-ing and rock-ing ba-by you're just as fine as you can be
Good-bye Claw-dy oh dar-ling down the road I'll go
B♭
C7
F
F6
B♭
Gm7
C7
F
3.4
5
4. Well now
5. Well so
Gm
F
Gm
F
Gm
C6
Gm
C7
F
B♭
B♭maj7
F

LITTLE SISTER

Words and Music by
Doc Pomus and Mort Shuman

Chorus
F
Lit-tle Sis-ter, don't you,
Lit-tle Sis-ter, don't you,
mf
Bb
Lit-tle Sis-ter, don't you kiss me once or twice Then say it's ver-y nice and then you
F
C7
Db7
run.
Lit-tle Sis-ter, don't you do what your big sis-ter
1.2.
F
C7
(Tacet)
3.
F
Bb7
F
done.
2. Ev - 'ry
3.Well, I
done.

LONG TALL SALLY

Words and Music by
Enotris Johnson, Richard Penniman and Robert Blackwell

Bb9
F
1.2.
3. (last time)
Hav-in' me some fun to-night. yeah! 2. Well, yeah! We're gon-na
3. Well, I
have some fun to-night, Gon-na have some fun to-night woo! We're gon-na
have some fun to-night, Ev-'ry-thing will be all right. We're gon-na
C7
Gm7
have some fun, gon-na have some fun to-night!

LOVE ME

Words and Music by
Jerry Leiber and Mike Stoller

I would beg and steal just to feel
your heart beat-ing close to mine.
Ev-'ry night I pray to the stars that shine a-bove me, Begging on my
knees, all I ask is please, please, love me. Treat me like a
G Tacet C G
A7 D7 A7
D7 G G7 C
1 2
D7 G C G G

LOVE ME TENDER

From the 20th Century-Fox Cinemascope Production 'Love Me Tender'

Words and Music by
Elvis Presley and Vera Matson

life com - plete, And I love you so.
I be - long, And we'll nev - er part.
all the years, Till the end of time.
fol - low you Ev - 'ry - where you go
A7 D7 sus4 D7 G
CHORUS
Love me ten - der, love me true, All my dreams ful -
mf
G B7 Em G7 C Cm
- fill For, my dar - lin', I love you,
G G Dm6 E7+ E7 A7
1
And I al - ways will.
D7 sus4 D7 G Am7 D7
2
And I al - ways will.
D7 sus4 D7 G

LOVING YOU

Featured by Elvis Presley in the Paramount Film 'Loving You'

Words and Music by
Mike Stoller and Jerry Leiber

lov - ing you. If I'm seen with some-one new, don't be blue,
C7 G7 C7 mp F C7
don't be blue. I'll be faith - ful I'll be true; al-ways true,
F
true to you. There is on - ly one for me, and you know who.
F7 mf B♭ F Cm6 D7
1 2
You know that I'll al-ways be lov - ing you. lov - ing you.
G7 C7 mp F Bdim C7 C7 rall. mp F

MEAN WOMAN BLUES

Words and Music by
Claude De Metruis

Medium Rock

1. A black cat up and died of fright, 'Cause she crossed his path last night. Oh,
2.(She) kiss so hard she bruise my lips. Hurts so good my heart just flips. Oh,
3.(The) strang-est gal I ev - er had; Nev - er hap - py 'less she's mad. Oh,
4. She makes love with - out a smile, Ooh hot dog, that drives me wild. Oh,
F Tacet
F Tacet
F Tacet
F7
I got a wom-an mean as she can be. Some-times I think she's
Bb7
F
C7
1.2.3.
4
al-most mean as me
2. She
3. The
4.
me. Some-
Bb7
F
F
-times I think she's al - most mean as me.
C7
Bb7
F

IN THE GHETTO

Words and Music by
Scott Davis

Em
F
G7
there's one thing she does-n't need_ It's an-oth-er hun-gry mouth_ to feed In The
C
G
Ghet-to._
Peo-ple, don't you un-der-stand, the child needs a
F
C
F
G7
help - ing hand,_ Or he'll grow to be an an - gry young man some-
C
F
C
C
F
C
G
day.
Take a look at you and me, Are we too

F7
C
F
Em
blind to see,
Or do we sim - ply turn our heads and
rit.
Dm
G7
C
F
C
F
C
look the oth - er way?
Well, the world turns
and a
a tempo
Em
F
G7
hun-gry lit-tle boy with the run - ny nose
Plays in the street as the cold wind blows In The
C
Ghet - to,
And his hun-ger burns

Em
And he starts to roam the streets at night And he
F G7 C
learns how to steal and he learns how to fight In The Ghet-to. And
G F C
then one night, in des-per-a-tion, a young man breaks a-way, He
F Em Dm G7
buys a gun, steals a car, tries to run, but he don't get far, and his

C F C F C Em
ma-ma cries.__ As a crowd gath-ers 'round an an - gry young man, face
F G7 C
down_ in the street with a gun_ in his hand_In The Ghet-to.__ And as her
C Em
young man dies, On a cold and gray Chi-ca - go morn-in', An-
F G7 C
oth-er lit-tle ba - by child_ is born_In The Ghet - to.__
rit.

MOODY BLUE

Words and Music by
Mark James

C7
F
___ to fig - ure out ___ what ___ she's all a - bout, ___ that she's a wo - man through and through.-
think I know her well, her e - mo - tions re - veal ___ she's not the per - son that I thought I knew._
G7
She's a com - pli - ca - ted la - dy, so co - lor my ba - by
C
G7
C
mood - y blue. ___
Oh, ___ mood - y blue, ___
tell me am I
Dm7
G7
get - tin' through. ___
I keep hang - in' on ___ try - na

C
G7
learn the song but I nev - er do.
Oh,
C
Dm7
mood - y blue,
tell me who I'm talk - in' to.
G7
You're like night and day, and it's hard to say which
C
1. Dm7
G7
2. G7
D.S. and fade
one is you.
(2) Well, when Mon -
Oh,

MONEY HONEY

Words and Music by
J. Stone

2. Well, I screamed and I hollered 'cos I'm so hard pressed,
I lost the woman that I loved the best;
I fin'ly reached my baby 'bout half past three
She said "Little baby, what was wrong with me?"
I cried

(To Chorus)

3. I learned my lesson, and now I know
The winds may come and the winds may go,
The women they come, and the women they go,
But how is it darlin' that you love me so?
She cried

(To Chorus)

MY BABY LEFT ME

Words and Music by
Arthur Crudup

3. Baby, one of these mornings, Lord, it won't be long,
You'll look for me and, Baby, and Daddy he'll be gone.
You know you left me, you know you left me.
My baby even left me, never said goodbye.

4. Now, I stand at my window, wring my hands and moan.
All I know is that the one I love is gone.
My baby left me, you know she left me.
My baby even left me, never said a word.

MYSTERY TRAIN

Words and Music by
Sam C. Phillips and Herman Parker Jr.

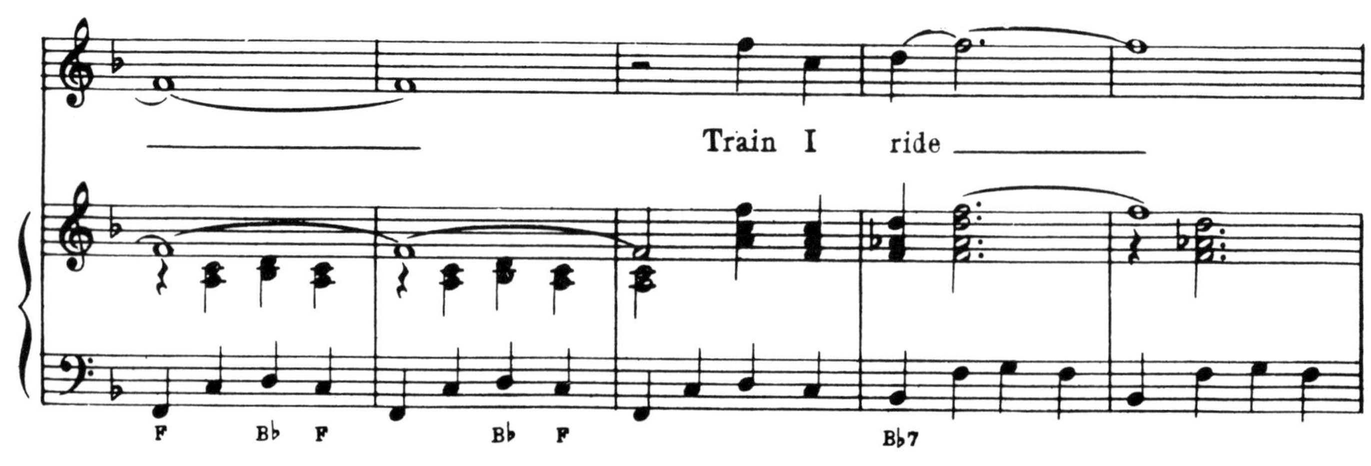

2. Train, train, coming 'round 'round the bend.
Train, train, coming 'round 'round the bend.
Well, it took my baby, well, it never will again
(no not again).

3. Train, train, coming down the line.
Train, train, coming down the line.
Well, it's bringing my baby 'cause she's mine, all mine
(she's mine, all mine).

MY BOY

Music by
Claude Francois and Jean-Pierre Bourtayre
Words by
Bill Martin and Phil Coulter

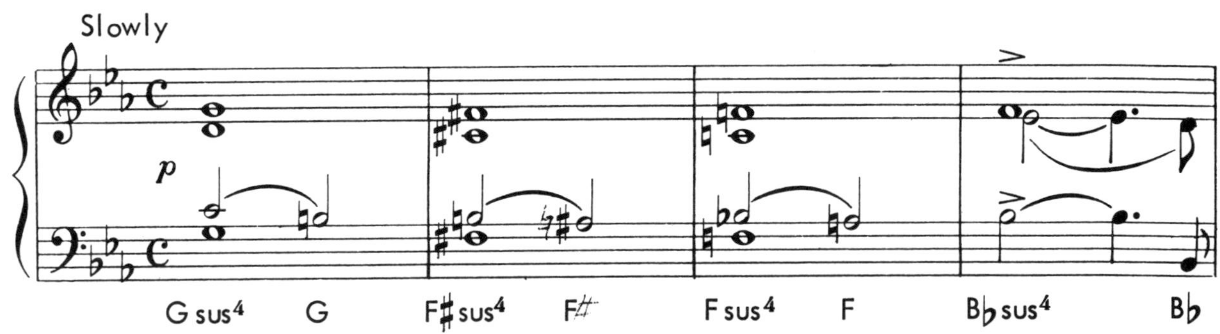

late.
part.
hell.
For your moth - er and
I have laughed, I have
Life is no fair - y
mf
Cm
me,
Love has fi - nal - ly
died;
This is no hap - py
cried;
I have lost ev -'ry
game,
Tak-en all I can
tale
As one day you will
know
But now you're just a
Ab
Gm
home
But God knows how I've
tried
Be-cause you're
take
But I'll stay just the
same
child
I'll stay here and watch you
grow
Fm
G7 sus 4
G7
Dm7
G7

all I have, my boy; You are my life, my pride my
Cm
Fm
B♭7
joy And if I stay, I stay be-cause of you, my
E♭
Am7-5
D7-9
D7
boy.
1,2
I
Sleep
G7 sus4
G7
E♭
3
D.𝄋 and Fade
know it's hard to un-der- Be-cause you're
on, you have-n't heard a
G7
Dm7
G7

OLD SHEP

Words and Music by
Clyde (Red) Foley

Moderato

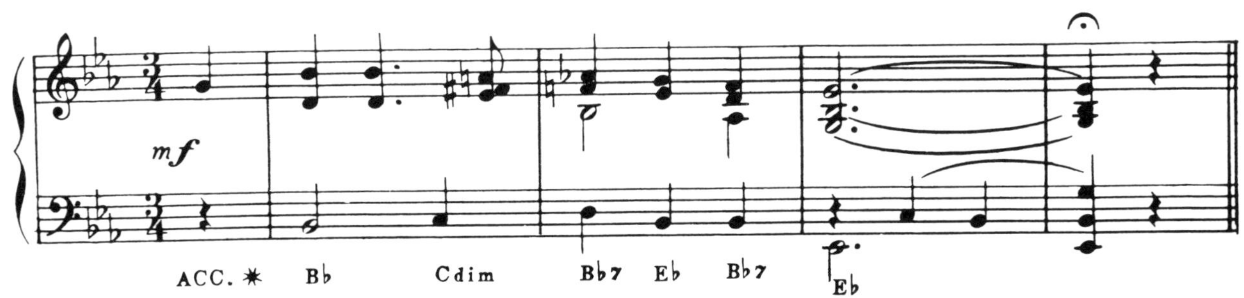

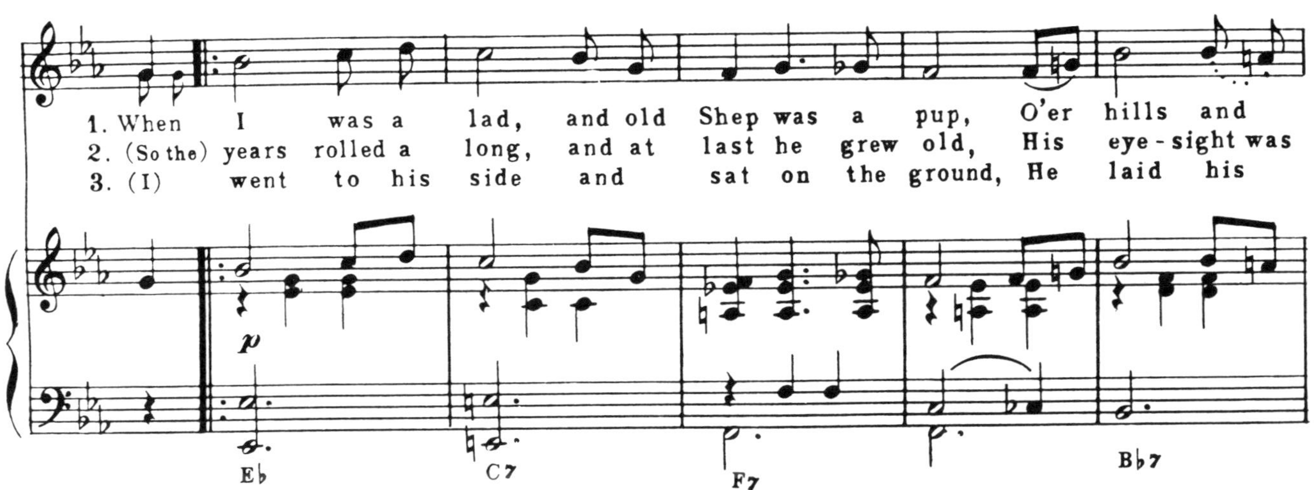

both full of fun We grew up to geth-er that way. I re-
at me and said I can't do no more for him, Jim. With a
man ev-er found I cried so I scarce-ly could see. Old
F7 B♭ Cdim B♭7 E♭ E♭7

-mem-ber the time at the old swim-ming hole, When I would have
hand that was tremb-ling I picked up my gun, I aimed it at
Shep-pie he knew he was go-ing to go, For he reached out and
A♭ E♭7 A♭m6 E♭

drowned be-yond doubt Shep was right there to the res-cue he
Shep's faith-ful head I just could-n't do it I want-ed to
licked at my hand He looked up at me, just as much as to
B♭dim B♭7 E♭ C7 F7

1. 2. 3
came He jumped in and helped pull me out. 2. So the
run And I wished that they'd shoot me in - stead. 3. I
say We're part - ing, but you un - der - stand. Now
Bb7 Cdim Bb7 Eb Cdim Bb7
Last time only
old Shep is gone, where the good dog - gies go And no more with old
Eb B7 Bb7 Eb Cm
Shep will I roam But if dogs have a heav - en, there's
F7 Bb7 Eb C7
one thing I know Old Shep has a won - der - ful home.
F7 Bb Cdim Bb7 Eb Bb7 Eb
Fine

ONE NIGHT

Words and Music by
Dave Bartholomew and Pearl King

C C7 F7 C
hide. Al-ways lived a ver-y qui-et life. I ain't nev - er did no
D7 G7 (tacet) G7+
wrong. Now I know that life with-out you has been too lone-ly too long. One night with
C Dm7 3 G7 Dm7 3 G7
you is what I'm now pray-ing for. The things that we two could plan
3 3
Dm7 G7 C F7 G7 (tacet) C F7 C
would make my dreams come true. One night with true.

PARALYZED

Words and Music by
Otis Blackwell and Elvis Presley

day, Ev-er since that day you came 'my way, You made my life for
C F C F
me just one big hap-py game. I'm gay ev-'ry morn-ing, at night I'm still the same. Do
C Am D7 G7 (Tacet) G7
you re-mem-ber that won-der-ful time You held my hand and swore that you'll be
C
mine? In front of the preacher you said, "I do!" I could-n't say a word for think-ing of you.
G7 C C7 F7
1 2
All I could do was stand there par-a-lyzed. -lyzed.
C G7 C C

READY TEDDY

Words and Music by
John Marascalo and Robert Blackwell

Bright Tempo

Read - y, set, go, man, go, I got a gal that I love so. I'm

f

Chorus

F7 C G7 F7 C (Tacet)

Read-y Read-y Read-y Ted - dy. I'm Read-y Read-y Read-y Ted - dy. I'm Read-y Read-y Read-y Ted - dy. I'm Read-y Read-y Read-y to - a rock 'n' roll

f

C (Tacet)
rock 'n' roll ba - by, she's the ap - ple of my eye, 'Cause I'm
Chorus
F7
C
Read - y Read - y Read - y Ted - dy. I'm Read - y Read - y Read - y Ted - dy. I'm
f
G7
F7
C (Tacet)
Read - y Read - y Read - y Ted - dy. I'm Read-y Read-y Read-y to - a rock 'n' roll.
Verse
C
(Tacet)
2. Well, the flat top cats and the dun - ga - ree dolls Are —
3. (Gon - na) kick off my shoes, roll — up my fad - ed jeans. Grab my
f

C (Tacet)
head-ed for the gym to the Sock Hop Ball._ The joint is real-ly jump-in', the
rock 'n' roll__ ba-by, pour_ on the steam. I shuf-fle to the left._ I
cats are go-in' wild._ The mu-sic real-ly sends me. I dig that cra-zy style, 'Cause I'm
shuf-fle to the right. Gon-na rock_ 'n'_ roll till the ear-ly ear-ly night, 'Cause I'm
Chorus
F7
G7
Read-y Read-y Read-y Ted-dy. I'm Read-y Read-y Read-y Ted-dy. I'm Read-y
Read-y Read-y Ted-dy. I'm Read-y Read-y Read-y to-a rock 'n' roll. 3. Gon-na rock 'n' roll.
f
ff

RETURN TO SENDER

Words and Music by
Otis Blackwell and Winfield Scott

F
G7
F
G7
ad - dress un - known.
No such num - ber,
C
1.
C7
F
G7
no such zone.
We had_ a quar - rel,
F
G7
D7
a lov - er's spat.
I write I'm sor - ry but my
G7
2. C
C7
F
let - ter keeps com - ing back.
zone.
This time I'm gon - na

F
C
D7
take it my-self and put it right in her hand. And if it comes back the
G7 (Tacet)
A F
ver-y next day, Then I'll un-der-stand_ the writ-ing on it. Re-turn_ to
G7
F
G7
F
send-er, ad-dress un-known. No such
G7
C
1. C
C7 Return to A
2. C
F7
C
num-ber, no such zone. zone._______

SHE'S NOT YOU

Words and Music by
Jerry Leiber, Mike Stoller and Doc Pomus

F
B♭
F
(Tacet)
A7
you.
And when we're danc - ing,
F7
B♭
it al - most feels the same. I've got to stop my - self from
A7 (Tacet)
C7 (Tacet)
F
whis - p'ring your name. She e - ven kiss - es me like you used to
C7
Cdim
C7
B♭
C7
do. And it's just break - ing my heart 'cause she's not
1. F
D♭7
C7
(Tacet)
2. F
B♭7
F
you. Her hair is you.

SO GLAD YOU'RE MINE

Words and Music by
Arthur Crudup

2. My baby knows just how to treat me right
   Gives me plenty lovin' morning, noon and night,
   She cries Oo - ee etc

3. When my baby does what she does to me
   I climb the highest mountain down in the deep blue sea,
   She cries Oo - ee etc

4. My baby's lips are red and sweet like wine,
   She let's me lay down in her lovin' arms all night,
   She cries Oo - ee etc

SUSPICION

Words and Music by
Doc Pomus and Mort Shuman

Dm
real - ly real - ly real - ly love me,
keep on caus - ing me such sor - row?
love will keep_ on grow - ing strong - er.
Dm
G7sus.4
C
(Tacet)
Do you speak the same words to some - one else_ when I'm not there?
Why am I so doubt - ful when - ev - er you_ are out of sight? Sus -
May - be I'm sus - pi - cious 'cause true love is_ so hard to find.
Chorus
Am
pi - cion_ tor - ments my heart._ Sus - pi - cion_ keeps us a - part._ Sus -
(Tacet)
1. D7♭5
G7 (Tacet)
pi - cion,_ why tor - ture me!_
2. D7♭5
G7 (Tacet)
C
A♭7
C
me!_ Why tor - ture me!_

TEDDY BEAR

Words and Music by
Kal Mann and Bernie Lowe

rough. I don't want to be your li - on 'cause li - ons ain't the kind you love e -
G7 F G7 F G7
- nough. Just wan - na be your Ted - dy Bear.
C Tacet C
Put a chain a - round my neck and lead me an - y - where. Oh, let me be
F C G7
1 2
your Ted-dy Bear. Bear.
Tacet C F7 G7 C F7 C

THAT'S ALL RIGHT

Words and Music by
Arthur Crudup

3. I'm leavin' town tomorrow, leavin' town for sure,
Then you won't be bothered with me hangin' 'round your door,
But that's all right, that's all right.
That's all right, mama, any way you do.

4. I oughta mind my papa, guess I'm not too smart.
If I was I'd leave you, go before you break my heart,
But that's all right, that's all right.
That's all right, mama, any way you do.

STUCK ON YOU

Words and Music by
Aaron Schroeder and J. Leslie McFarland

C7
C7+
Bb7
F (tacet)
stick like glue, Stick be-cause I'm Stuck on
stick like glue, Stick be-cause I'm Stuck on
1.
C7
2.
Bb
you. you. Hide in the kitch-en, hide in the hall.
F
Bb
Ain't gon-na do you no good at all. 'Cause once I catch ya and the
Bb
C7 (tacet)
kiss-in' starts, A team o' wild hors-es could-n't tear us a-part.

F
Try to take a ti - ger from his dad-dy's side. That's _ how _ love is gon - na
F Bb7
keep us tied. _ Uh-huh-huh. _ Yes-sir - ee, _ uh - huh. _
F C7 C7+
I'm gon- na stick like glue, _
Bb7 F (tacet) 1. C7 2. F
Yay, yay, _ be-cause I'm Stuck on you. you.

TRYING TO GET TO YOU

Words and Music by
Rose Marie McCoy and Charles Singleton

true, I've been trav'-lin' night and day, I've been run-nin' all the
do, I would trav-el night and day, and I'd still run all the
F
way, Ba-by try-in' to get to you. When I read your lov-in'
way, Ba-by try-in' to get to you. There was noth-in' that could
Fm
C
C7
let-ter, then my heart be-gan to sing,
hold me or could keep me 'away from you,
F7
C
There were man-y miles be-tween us, But they did-n't mean a
When your lov-in' let-ter told me that you real-ly loved me
C7
F

thing. I just had to reach you, Ba - by
true. Lord a - bove, you know I love you,
D7 (5♭) G7 tacet * C
spite of all that I've been through.
It was He that brought me through.
I kept trav-'lin' night and
When my way was dark at
day, I kept run - nin' all the way, Ba - by, try - in' to get to
night, He would shine His bright - est light, when I was try - in' to get to
F Fm
1 you. I've been trav-'lin' o-ver
you.
2 you.
C (tacet) * C

THERE GOES MY EVERYTHING

Words and Music by
Dallas Frazier

Chorus
Bb F7 Bb F7 Bb Bb7
There goes my rea - son for liv - ing,
mf
Eb F7 Bb F7 Bb
There goes the one of my dreams,
There goes my
Bb7 Eb Bb F7
on - ly pos - ses - sion,
There Goes My Ev - 'ry -
1. Bb F7
thing.
2. As my
2. Bb
thing.
mp
ritard.

TOO MUCH

Words and Music by
Lee Rosenberg and Bernard Weinman

Medium Rock

1
2.3
To A
I do all the giv-in' 'Cause I love you too much.
leave me bro-ken heart-ed 'Cause I love you too much.
tho' I know you're ly-in' 'Cause I love you too much.
Eb7
Bb
Tacet
Tacet
Need your lov-in' all the time. Need your hug-gin' please, be mine. Need you near me;
Bb
Eb7
stay real close. please, please, hear me, you're the most. Now you got me start-ed don't you
Bb
F7
1 Return to Chorus
2
leave me bro-ken heart-ed 'Cause I love you too much. much.
Eb7
Bb
Tacet

TREAT ME NICE

Words and Music by
Jerry Leiber and Mike Stoller

real-ly gon-na freeze. If you don't want me to be cold as ice, Treat me
G7 C D7 G7 (Tacet)
nice. Make me feel at home If you real-ly care. Scratch my back and
C C7 F C F F♯dim7 C F
run your pret-ty fin-gers through my hair, You know I'd be your slave, If you ask me
C C+ F F♯ G7 C C
to. But if you don't be-have, I'll walk right out on you. If you want my love then
C7 F G7
take my ad - vice. Treat me nice. When nice.
1 2
D7 G7 (Tacet) C F7 G7 C F7 C

TUTTI FRUTTI

Words and Music by
R. Penniman, D. La Bostrie and Joe Lubin

VERSE
RECORD VERSES
POP VERSES
1. I got a gal (guy) her (his) name's Sue (Lou) She (he) knows just what to do
2. I got a gal (guy) her (his) name's Dai - sy (Jackie) She (he) al - most drives me cra - zy (wacky)
3. I got - ta go, can't stop, Down to the can - dy shop
4. You're the one I miss, I got - ta tell you this
5. Won't you be my date, And ba - by, don't be late
I got a gal (guy) her (his) name's Sue (Lou) She (he)
I got a gal (guy) her (his) name's Dai - sy (Jackie) She (he)
I got - ta go, can't stop, And
Oh, you're the one I miss, And the
Oh, won't you be my date, And
knows just what to do. I've been to the east, I've
al - most drives me cra - zy. (wacky) She's (he's) a real gone cook - ie,
get me an ice cream pop. Don't want va - nil - la or
fla - vor of your kiss. I don't mean cher - ry with
share my ice - cream plate. With - out your kis - ses,

been to the west, But she's (he's) the gal (guy) I love the best.
yes - sir - ree, But pret - ty lit - tle Su - zy's the gal (guy) for me.
(coo - ool lit - tle Lou - ie's)
straw - ber - ry too, Want the same kind of fla - vor when I'm kiss - ing you. TUT - TI
choc - 'late chips, I mean the same fla - vor of your sweet lips.
This is all I've got, Just an im - i - ta - tion fla - vor of you know what.
CHORUS
FRUT-TI au rut-ti TUT-TI FRUT-TI au rut-ti TUT-TI
FRUT-TI au rut-ti TUT-TI FRUT-TI au rut-ti TUT-TI FRUT-TI au
rut-ti A - bop - bop a - loom - op a - lop bop boom! 2. I got a
3. I got - ta
4. You're the
5. Won't you lop bop boom!

UNTIL IT'S TIME FOR YOU TO GO

Words and Music by
Buffy Sainte-Marie

space in the lives that we planned,
stayed out - side my heart but in you came,
G
G/F#
G/F♮
To Coda
and here we'll stay un - til it's time for you to
and here you'll stay un - til it's time for you to
E7
Am7
D7
1
2
go.
Yes we're
go.
G
G
Don't ask
why,
A♭
F7
G

Don't ask how,
A♭
F7
G
Don't ask for - ev - er.
B
B7
Em
Love me now.
This love of
Em
A7
D7
mine had no be - gin - ning it has no end.
I was an
G
G/F♯
G/F♮
E7

oak, now I'm a wil - low, now I can bend, and tho' I'll
Am
D7/F#
nev-er in my life see you a - gain, still I'll
G
G/F#
G/F♮
E7
stay un - til it's time for you to go.
Am7
D7
G
Don't ask why of me,
A♭
F7
G

Don't ask how of me,
A♭
F7
G
Don't ask for - ev - er of me,
B7
Em
D. S. al Coda
Love me, love me now. You're not a
A7
D7 sus4
D7
CODA
stay un - til it's time for you to go.
Am7
D7
G

WAY DOWN

Words and Music by
Layng Martine, Jr.

- tance
ly - in' on the floor
me, no doc - tor could pres - cribe your
B♭
F7
send - ing me to plac - es I've nev - er been be - fore.
love is do - in' some - thing that I just can't des - cribe.
C
G7
Ooh and I can feel it, feel it, feel
cresc.
C
Dm/C
tacet
G7
Chorus
it, feel it,
Way down where the mu - sic plays,
G7

way down like a ti - dal wave. Way down where the fir - es blaze, way
C
G7
down. down, way, way on
F
C
Dm/A
C/G
F
G7
1.
2
down, (way on down)
down)
C
Hold me a - gain as tight
C

as you can, I need you so, so ba - by let's go (way down) way down where it
G7
feels so good. Way down where I hoped it would. Way down where I
C
G7
nev - er could, way down, down,
F
C
Dm/A
C/G
Way, way on down, (way on down, way on down)
rall.
F
G7
C

WEAR MY RING AROUND YOUR NECK

Words and Music by
Bert Carroll and Russell Moody

1.
C
F
C
(Tacet)
2. C
F7
C7
F7
neck. Won't you wear my neck. They say that go-ing
C
C7
F7
stead-y is not the prop-er thing. They say that we're too young to know the
C
C7
F7
C
mean-ing of a ring. I on-ly know I love you and that you love me
D7
G7
D7-5
G7
(Tacet)
too. So, dar-ling, please do what I ask of you. Won't you wear my

C
ring a-round your neck To tell the world
G7
C
C7
I'm yours, by heck.
Let them see your love for
Let them know I love you
F
C
G7
(Tacet)
me, And let them see by the ring a-round your
so, And let them know by the ring a-round your
1.C
F7
G7
(Tacet)
neck. Won't you wear my
2.C
F7
C
neck.

WHEN MY BLUE MOON TURNS TO GOLD AGAIN

Words and Music by
Wiley Walker and Gene Sullivan

B♭
F7
F7
E♭
F7
day they'll live a - gain, sweet - heart, And my
dreams they live a - gain, sweet - heart, But my
we will live them all a - gain, And my
F6
F7
B♭
E♭
B♭
blue moon a - gain will turn to gold.
gol - den moon is just a mem - o - ry.
blue moon a - gain will turn to gold.
CHORUS
B♭
F7
F7
WHEN MY BLUE MOON TURNS TO GOLD A - GAIN, When the
mf

B♭
rain - bow turns the clouds a - way; WHEN MY
B♭ F7 F7 E♭ F7
BLUE MOON TURNS TO GOLD A - GAIN, You'll be back in my
F6 G6m F7 B♭ E♭6 B♭ B♭ E♭ B♭
1:2.
Fine
arms to stay. 2. The stay.
3. The
D.S. al Fine
mp
rit.

WILD IN THE COUNTRY

Words and Music by
George Weiss, Hugo Peretti and Luigi Creatore

Gm F Bb Am G7 C7
deer_ and the dove. Wild and free_ is this land_ that I love. A
F Bb C7
dream grows wild_ in the coun - try.___ A love grows tall_ as the
F F Bb
sky.___ A heart beats wild_ in the coun - try,___ And
C7 F C7
here_ with a dream_ in my heart, Part_ of the wild, wild
Bb C7 1. F 2. F
coun - try am I. A I.___
rall.
Ped.

WOODEN HEART

Words and Music by
Fred Wise, Ben Weisman, Kay Twomey and Berthold Kaempfert

don't have a wood - en heart. There's no strings up-
Fm7 Bb7 Eb Ab Eb Fm
- on this love of mine, It was al - ways you from the start,
Bb7 Eb Ab Eb E°
Treat me nice, treat me good, treat me like you real-ly should, 'Cause
Bb7 Eb Fm7 Bb7 Eb Ab Eb
I'm not made of wood, And I don't have a wood - en heart.
Eb Ab Eb Fm7 Bb7 Eb Ab Eb

11/96(26291)